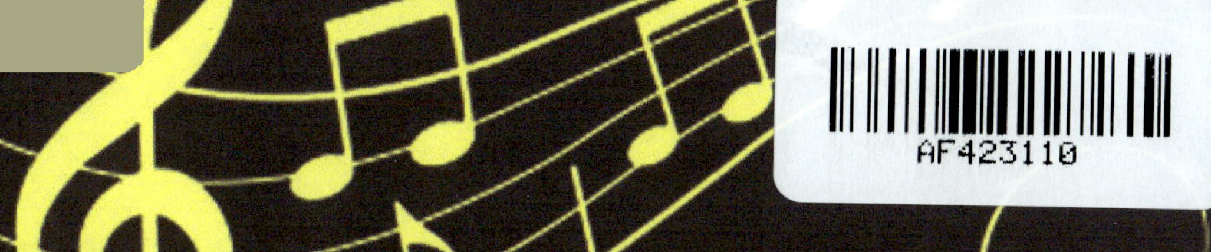

GIVE THE DRUMMER SOME

DRUM LINE ORIGINS IN SCHOOL-DAZE CONFUNKTORY

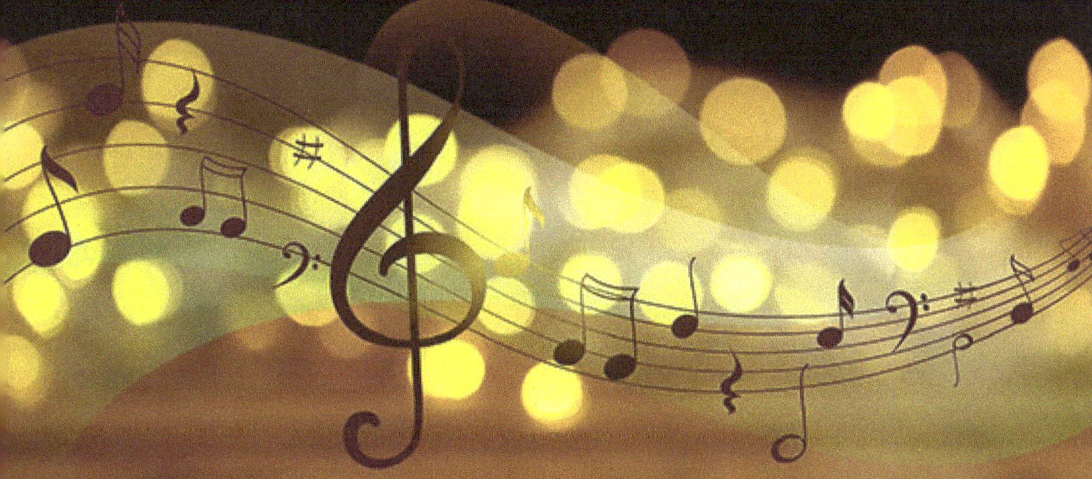

MILTON LAWRENCE COX II

Give the Drummer Some

Drumline Origins in School-Daze Confunktory

by

MILTON LAWRENCE COX II

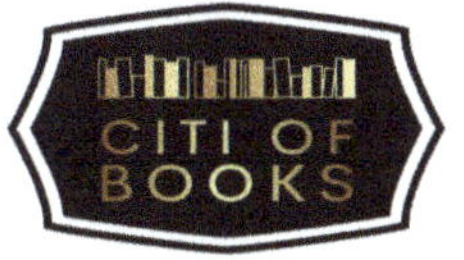

CITIOFBOOKS, INC.
3736 Eubank NE Suite A1
Albuquerque, NM 87111-3579
www.citiofbooks.com
Hotline: 1 (877) 389-2759
Fax: 1 (505) 930-7244

Ordering Information:
Quantity sales. Special discounts are available on quantity purchases by corporations, associations, and others. For details, contact the publisher at the address above.

Printed in the United States of America.
ISBN-13:   Paperback   979-8-89391-107-7
               eBook   979-8-89391-108-4

Library of Congress Control Number: 2024909500

TABLE OF CONTENTS

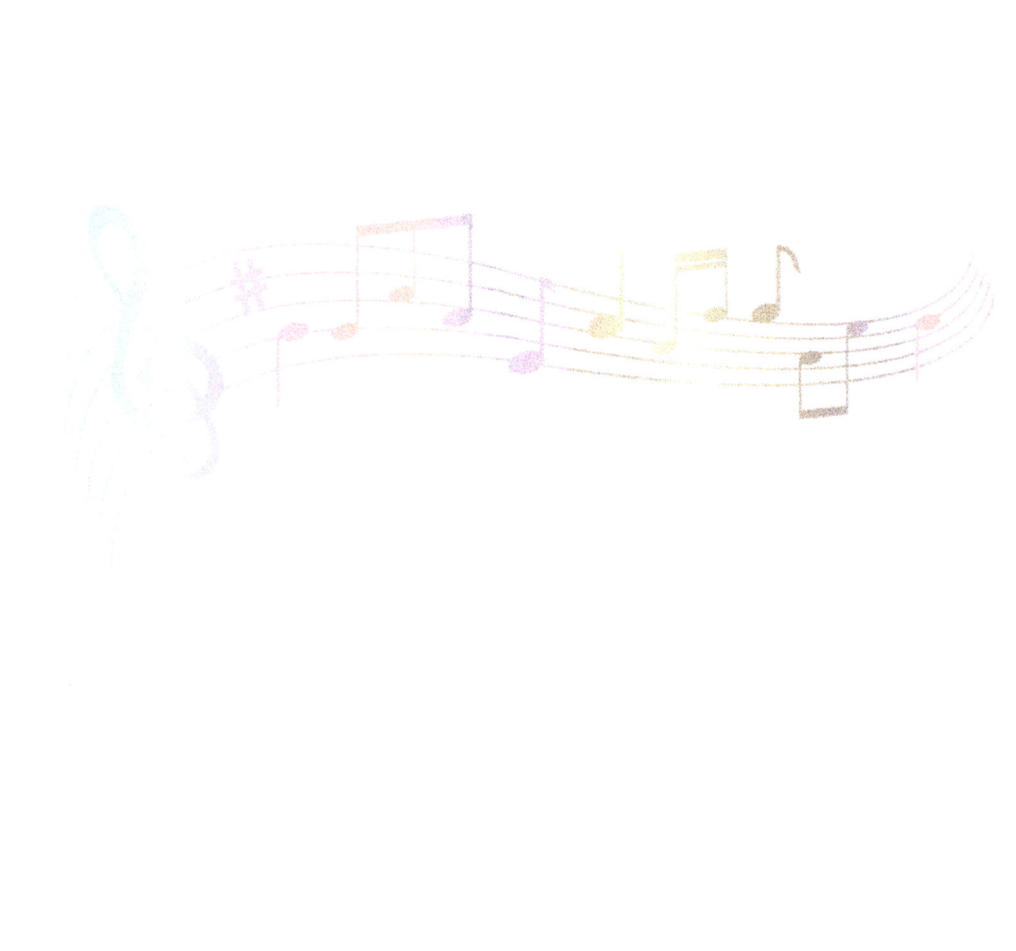

Kudos! To you, Milton Cox, for taking the time to write about an outstanding era in our lives. The reading of your manuscript was an easy read, fun, informative, interesting and the whole truth.

While reading the manuscript, I could vividly remember my time in the marching bands of S.H. Clarke Junior High School, I.C. Norcom High School of Portsmouth, VA, and Virginia State College, Petersburg, VA. I was a member of the flute section. Throughout our entire marching band experience, we were taught the heartbeat of the band was the percussion section that we now call the "drumline."

As a member of the "Marching 110" of Virginia State, we were drilled on how to perform, to listen, to articulate the shows and how to be a part of a team. Everybody loved the drummers because they were so cool and serious and carried the band as a unit. I still remember the beats.

To this day as I return to Virginia State University for homecoming, I must see the half time show and watch the band execute their shows. Sometimes I still try to march a little bit on the sidelines despite my age.

The "HBCU Marching Bands" are cohesive units that thrive on working together for the common cause as a unit. As Milton spotlights the "drumline," I do remember their dominance at the games. On many occasions, the flute section happened to end up sitting in front of the drummers in the stands. We were told not to speak and watch the game. We obeyed because the drummers said so.

This book can be used as a teaching tool on all educational levels. To be a member of a marching band takes perseverance, dedication, and a love for your fellow band members.

Milton Cox has crossed every "T" and dotted every "I" in this manuscript. I wish you the best in your future endeavors and the success of your book, "Give the Drummer Some."

O, How I remember!!!

Submitted by:
Julia Wiggins-Hughey
S.H. Clarke Junior High School 1963-1965
I.C. Norcom High School 1965-1969
Virginia State College 1969-1973

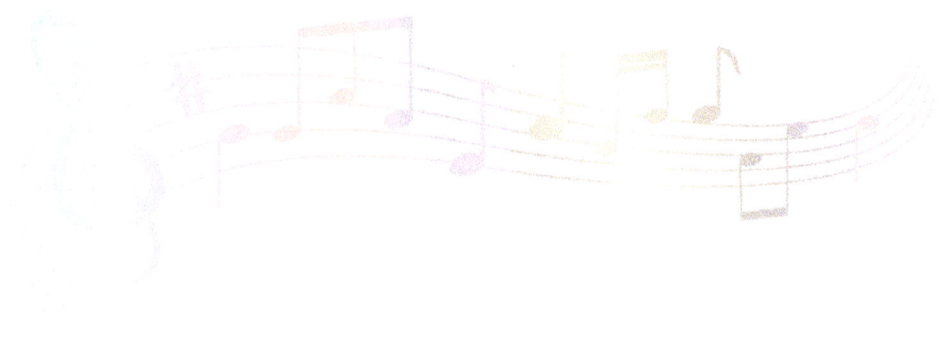

Acknowledgments

I'd like to acknowledge all of the drummers, the guys and gals, that I met and forged friendships with all for the sake of developing our skills, 1st as "marching band drummers", and 2ndly as "concert band and jazz band percussionists."

Special thanks to those persons who assisted as manuscript readers, Truxtun Group, who aided with their constructive grammatical insight for overall cohesiveness and flow of this project: Annette Brocket; Randall Eley; William Hayes; Lionel Hines; Julia Wiggins Hughley; and Verrandall Tucker.

Thanks also to those music persons, the band directors, and orchestra directors who gave their time and energy to infuse discipline of a musical compass and structure into the lives of young student "school-daze musicians."

ABOUT THE BOOK'S TITLE

Popularized and coined by Soul Brother #1, James Brown, "The Hardest Working Man in Show Business"… His well-oiled band of funk, the Famous Flames, and later the J.B.'s featured solos by Maceo Parker on Saxophone and Fred Wesley on Trombone. James would cue the drum solo, John "Ja Bo" Starks (1975-1979) by calling out "gea-da-drumma-sum"!

Mr. Brown made the 1-3 beat a staple in Funk music with his band's rendition of "Cold Sweat" (1967) and "Make It Funky, Pt. 1" (1971).

Listeners would groove to the funky sounds of the "Godfather of Soul" on the local Hampton Roads radio stations at WHIH and WRAP.

Live performances of James Brown with his famous band were enjoyed at Sunset Lake Park in the Deep Creek area of Chesapeake; the Arena in Norfolk and the Pavilion in Portsmouth.

FROM THE AUTHOR...

"Give the Drummer Some" is written from the actual life experiences of African American school boy drummer, Milton Lawrence Cox II.

Cox, a native of Portsmouth, VA, gives a personal insight into his school-daze adventures as a junior high schooler, high schooler, and ccollegian "snare-drummer" in the "marching-band", "concert-band", and "string-orchestra". Cox gives us a snapshot into some of the events which help transition a regular "marching-band drum-section" to what is known as the "Drumline."

"Give the Drummer Some" is an exposition as to some of the events and circumstances of the late 1960s and early 1970s "African-American HBCU (Historical Black College and University) marching-band units," which led to the transition of the "drum section" to the "drumline."

What moved the "drum-section format toward the "drumline" format was **(1)** a competitive edge among percussionists, **(2)** a desire to challenge and push the envelope of "rudimentar- cadences", and **(3)** a movement to know something musically and personally of the rival school's percussion section."This was an up-close, look-em-in-the-eye, square-off, volley moment of drum-section to drum-section!!. It transitioned from a "military-style-cadence" to a "funk-beat-syncopated" style cadence, to a funk-beat style cadence, from a "stagnant-type drum-section" that didn't have much movement.

It was paramount for each drummer to move and play while in motion, for there were crowds gathered to see!!!

The crowds that we encountered at "Big State" and beyond inspired us and hyped us up—made us play better. They seemed to crave/sense some euphoric elation of grandeur. In the "drumline" segment, we knew that we had the undivided attention of the crowd. We entertained them, and they made us play better, happier, funkier, livelier, and distinct in our confunktory. It was us and them, one-on-one, up close. No, we didn't back the crows off of us or try to move them out of the way. They could gather around us and encircle us up close, in some sense touching and feeling the vibes with their taste buds.

They drew off of our energy and the "drum-section" drew off of their inquisitive confunktory interests. They were in wonderment of what the drum-section would do next, and we made it our goal as a "drum-section" to be a creatives as possible with our routines.

The crowds would grow while we were performing. We would start a "beginning-cadence" with one crowd, and by the time we started the "second cadence", it was a whole new, larger crowd.

When the crowds saw us, smiling at each other and nodding at each other's approval, and looking them in their eyes, we knew that we were on the "cutting-edge" of "percussion performance."

DEDICATION

"Someone's got to tell about what we did up here," on "the Hill," far above the Appomattox in the early "1970s VSU-Legendary-Marching-110-Band."

I expressed this in a conversation with one of my bass drum players, Mike Thrift, during Homecoming games circa 1999 and 2000, at the back-gate where he was monitoring the V.I.P. entrance to Rogers Stadium on campus.

For me, it all began as I transitioned from elementary school to junior high school in the mid-1960s when the Motown Movement was beginning to crescendo.

Now drummers, come with me and turn your "sheet music" to begin this journey as I present our account of performing as "innovative, cutting-edge, high-stepping marching-band-percussionists."

To the guys and gals that I was privileged to meet and associate with musically when our focus was on honing our skills as "percussion-drummers..."

Special kudos to the two legendary "VSU Marching 110" bookend bass drummers par excellent, **Michael Thrift** and **Calvin Powell**... THANKS...

The "Toilet-Stool" position just keeps on rolling....

Por Rump Pum Pum Pum !!!

LETTER TO THE AUTHOR

2/12/2015

Dear Lawrence,

Thank you for opportunity to read your manuscript. I was truly blessed because I was taken back to the days at VSU that I had forgotten. This is entertaining, as it informs. Gosh, I learned so much about drums and drummers.

"Tidewater Slim" was on the campus when I was a student, and I knew personally a number of the people mentioned. Emery Fears was my neighbor in Deep Creek for many years.

I think every former member of the "Marching 110" would love to have the book.

Best regards to you, and save me my autographed copy!

Annette Brocket
VSU, Majorette Alumnus, 1961-1962;
 Clarinet, 1962-1965

DOWN-BEAT

As a "percussion-player" and more speciffically a "marching-band-snare-drum-player" by designation, talent, and trade, I really enjoyed the experience of watching the movie "Drumline," which came out in 2002. True to the techniques and teachings of a "college-level-marching-band-snare-drummer, "Drumline" epitomized the struggle and sheer grit that it takes to participate in a "Drum-Section" at a Historical Black College." "Drumline" dipicted a drummer when he or she has reached the apex of many hours of practicing stick-action, memorizing and creating cadences, and developing and fine-tuning sectional routines. It didn't start there, and this is my personal angle on bringing this experience in from a "beginner-drummer" to "drumline-professional."

As I wacthed "Drumline", I began to realize that there is a good argument that my "Drum-Section" at Virginia State University in Petersburg, VA, from 1971through 1973 possibly was responsible for starting and initiating the "Drum-Section" competition which isnow known as "the Drumline." It is my desire that these pages will shed light on this assertion and add some historical light to musical aspirations and cravings for the young men and women who perform as "drummers-on-the-brink."

Acknowledgments

This book is dedicated to the ladies and gentlemen who served as band and orchestra directors during my formative educational school years. I thank them for their tireless energy in sharing their time, offering instruction, and instilling in students a sense of dedication to the work ethic required to strive for excellence in musical bandmanship and in life.

Charles Jenkins, Sr.
James "Poochie" Mallory
Band directors, S. H. Clarke Junior High School
Portsmouth, VA

Jerlene Harding
Orchestra Conductor, S. H. Clarke Junior High School
Cradock High School
Tidewater Area Musicians (TAM Orchestra)
Portsmouth, VA

William P. Barley
Band Director, Cradock High School
Portsmouth, VA

Claiborne "Sticks" Richardson
Oneil Sanford
Band directors, Virginia State University
Petersburg, VA

CHAPTER 1

Me and Baby Brother

It all began with me in elementary school, in the 6th grade in 1963. All 6th graders at Truxtun Elementary School in Portsmouth, VA, were required to take a music test for the band or the chorus as we approached entering junior high school. My test results for the band came back with high marks in playing the clarinet and in playing the percussion or drum instruments. I had the opportunity to choose one of those instruments. My decision was to play the percussion. I based my decision to play the percussion (drum) instrument versus playing the clarinet because, for me, the percussion was a more masculine instrument. I later discovered that there were a few males playing the clarinet in the marching band.

In 1964, as a 7th grade "marching-band" member at S. H. Clarke Junior High School in Portsmouth, VA. I started out with the "beginner-drummers" during the summer band practices just before the school year would begin. "Beginner-drummers" would learn and practice percussion-rudiments on rubber drum-pads. We had to personally purchase a "Drum-Pad" and "Drum--Sticks," usually the large 3A type sticks. Percussion practice of the rudiments meant learning the bases of drum beats, which included the "single stroke", "the flam", "flam accent", "closed roll","open roll", "paradiddle", "ratamacue", & "flam tap."

All of the rudiment beats were to be played and practiced on the "Drum-Pad." "Beginner-drummers" could not use a real drum but could only use the "drum-pad," which had a circle in the middle of the pad in which the drummer was to focus all of their strokes without their sticks touching as they met together in the circle.

"Beginner-drummers" didn't like playing on those "drum-pads" All of us were anxious to play the real drums. Also, it wasn't fashionable to be seen playing on the"drum-pad." Students who saw you with the "drum-pad" had to be given an explanation as to why you weren't playing the drums yet. It was awkward just to start explaining that to someone. You could show them your "drum-sticks" but that wasn't good enough. They would put you in the category of second string. They wanted to know and to see that you were playing real drums.

During summer band practice, all "beginner-drummers" had to assemble in the chorus room, which was next to the band room sectioned off with their own wing of the building for the music department. All alone in the chorus room, drummers brought their "drum pad" and "snare-drum" sticks to practice their "rudiments." Some pads were flat, round pieces of black rubber with a circle in the middle that sat contour to the table top, and some were black squares of rubber mounted on angular blocks of wood.

For many band practices, that's all "beginner drummers" did was to assemble in the chorus room and practice "rudiments." It weeded out those who really wanted to learn how to play the drums from those who were there just for the glitter and fanfare of being associated with playing in a school's "Marching-Band-Drum-Section," I call them "wannabe-drummers." They don't really have the drummer skill, but they just want to be in the "drum-section" an hang around the drummers.

"Beginner-marching-band-drummer" were also taught the proper way to hold the "snare-drum-sticks". The right hand held the drum stick as if you were going to pick up a stick to throw. The left hand held the other drum stick laying it across the hand between the third and fourth finger with the thumb giving it balance. Each "beginner-drummer" was taught to hold their "snare drum sticks" in a light manner using a type of "wrist-action" along with high-stick-action or "bounce" to generate your "stroke-control" and power for the desired volume. Volume and power were controlled by your stick-action. Stick-action means that on every beat, your wrist lifts the drum stick up off of that stroke in preparation for the coming beat. The "Flam" rudiment was excellent in teaching and demonstrating the "high-stick-action" technique.

Once the "rudiments" were learnd,, tests were given. As each beginning drummer had to demonstrate on the drum pad the rudiments accompanied with whatever stick-action and wrist action

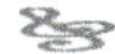

that was comfortable for the drummer. The "beginner-drummer" that demonstrated the better stick and wrist-action along with sustaining a single stroke roll and able to play with your focus centered in the middle of the drum pad were assigned snare drums. The beginner drummer that demonstrated the not-so-comfortable stick and wrist-action were assigned tenor drums; the larger fellows were assigned the bass drum, or they just usually gravitated to them.

In junior high school, snare and tenor drums were carried with a single white drum strap which ran across the chest, over one shoulder and along the back as the drum rested just above the right knee. The bass drummers used a shoulder harness where each shoulder went through straps to hold their drums up. Initially the snare drum was somewhat cumbersome and awkward to get control of while marching. As you marched, it would move all around your leg, from side to side. Some of the drummers would use string or raw hide to tie their drums around their legs to hold them in place. Later they did away with the string because they wanted the free movement of their drums. Also the "snare-drummer" or "tenor-drummer" couldn't take a regular step with that "drum-leg."

It was strange being a "beginner-drummer" because from the beginning you hadn't become a part of the band as a whole. The beginner-drummer was relugated to only practicing on that "drum-pad" with fellow "beginner-drummers" We practiced individually and as a group, usually in the chorus room during summer band practices and a couple of the drummers would come to my house to practice "rudimens."

The school year started in the fall, in September, but it was still hot as if it were summer, as it usually was here in Hampton Roads, VA. It was a hot day in August when I learned the meaning of being a drummer and a "drummer-on-the-brink." The entire band had finished practicing sectional parts in the band room, and the band director asked the drummers to go outside. Each section practiced sheet music. The band room was located in the back of the school with its own back door exit to the outside. The entire "drum-section" went outside and walked about 50 yards across the back of the school yard with instruments in hand. It was so hot that we thought that we shouldn't have been out there, but we gathered under a huge tree that bore plenty of shade. There under that tree is where we began to learn the different cadences as they were taught to us by the 8th grade drummers. We pacticed and learned those "cadences" for a session that felt like time didn't exist. The band director allowed us to go out there by ourselves to work out our own "drum-section--chemistry." During that practice is where stamina and skill came together to take that "beginner-marching-ban-drummer" on the journey of always being "on-the-brink" of some rhythm syncopation. We practiced and practiced and wrote in our memory those basic "drum-cadences" to get us started in the art-of- being that "specialized-percussion-musician." When we returned to the band room the rest of the band had long departed for home.

My parents purchased a "concert-snare-drum" with a stand to play the "snare-drum" on for me to practice at home. I incorporated my practices with the "rubber-drum-pad," which covered the entire "snare-hide." I closed my room door to help reduce the noise entering the rest of the house. I used that "snare-drum-pad," some of the time, but there were other times when I removed the "drum-pad" and turned my stereo up and practiced alongside the rhythms from the current hit musical artists. In my room, I focused on stick placement in the center of the drum hide, "wrist-action", and "rudiment" strengthening.

During summer band practice clarinet and other woodwind players had to work on having the proper embouchure with the mouthpiece of their instrument. Embouchure is the position and use of one's lips on the mouthpiece in producing a musical tone on a woodwind instrument. Woodwind players practiced proper embouchure for hours. I like playing the drums because drummers didn't have to worry about embouchure or use their breath to blow an instrument in their mouth.

Being in the "marching-band" at S. H. Clarke Junior High School, with an all "African-American" student body, had added pressure in that the school was located in the shadow, diagonally across the street from one of the premier "African-American" high schools in the country. I. C. Norcom was so popular that its band achieved and maintained "legendary-status" long before I entered junior high school or even thought about playing in a "marching-band." Most of Clarke's band students aspired to go to Norcom and to get in its band upon completion of junior high school. Norcoms' band had a following, that you could say, encompassed all of the "African- American" residents of Portsmouth. Just by being in the neighborhood of Norcom raised our excitement and challenged us as to how good we could be as a band and as a "drum-section." With the marching Greyhounds of I. C. Norcom High School as the premier band in the 757, Portsmouth became the "marching-band-mecca."

Drummers had to have stamina and had to maintain a good degree of stamina in all of the marching band performances. The "drum-section" was responsible for moving the band wherever it moved as a unit, and it had to play on all songs performed by the band. Therefore, drummers had to maintain stamina and play their instrument for the entirety of the marching performance.

Marching band performances, for the most part on the junior high school level, consisted of marching in the numerous parades in their city. Our band directors were very popular, that being Charles S. Jenkins and later James "Poochie" Mallory, were always getting invitations for the band to march in the various holiday parades. I. C. Norcoms' band director, Emery Fears, took Clarke's band under his wing and invited the band to perform halftime shows at Norcoms' football games. Through that relationship with the band directors, Clarke's band became the little brother of Norcoms' band and were very close to them. We touted ourselves as "the Baby Greyhounds." That praise inspired us to elevate ourselves in our overall performance presentation, beyond that of the typical junior high school band.

It got to the point that whenever Norcoms' band went to perform, we wanted to be right there with them. We wanted to be on the scene with the Greyhounds. We knew that by performing where Norcom was performing would elevate our skill level and enhance our overall confidence. We wanted to raise our performance level to Norcoms' level, and we were successful in doing that. It was such a confidence booster that when we had performances when Norcoms' band wasn't in attendance, we would steal the show from the other bands and outperform them. S. H. Clarkes' band, for a junior high school band, was no joke. We had progressed so much in two years, we felt that we could hold our own with any junior high or high school band, and we did.

The memorable parades were the Portsmouth City Christmas Parade, the Fish Bowl Parade, followed by attendance later that day of the Fish Bowl Classic football game at Portsmouth's Frank D. Lawrence Stadium, and Portsmouth's Memorial Day Parade, the oldest Memorial Day parade in the country, which began in 1884. Portsmouth's Christmas Parade began at Frank D. Lawrence Stadium and proceeded up High Street ending at Mid- City Shopping Center. Once the band made the turn into Mid-City Shopping Center with the throngs of people lining both sides of the street, the percussion section would get an extra boost of adrenaline, and bring our cadences to a crescendo. We knew that we had to try to steal the excitement before Norcoms' band would turn the corner.

During the Portsmouth Christmas Parade, Santa Claus wasn't allowed to be the last float. Usually, Santa Claus is the last float in the Christmas Parade. In this instance, if Santa was allowed to be the last float, the parade would have been over before he reached the parades' end. For this parade, Santa Claus's float was placed in the middle of the parade line up. He would precede S. H. Clarke's band, which was immediately in front of I. C. Norcoms' band.

Once the parade route wound down to the end, Santa Claus was already stationed in his perch at the center of Mid-City Shopping Center when Clarke's band and Norcoms' band turned the corner into the shopping center. Lines of children to see Santa had already formed at Santas' station in the middle of the parking lot of the shopping center. As Clarke made the turn, then Norcom, the throngs of people who had followed from the time Norcom stepped off from Frank D. Lawrence Stadium to the end were right on Norcoms' heals. People of high school students, elementary and junior high students ran the entire route following behind Norcoms' band. After Norcom came through, they would shut the parade down with their huge following. Swarms of children followed with shouts of joy and wide eyes taking in the excitement of Norcoms' parade performance from start to finish.

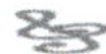

They would run behind the band, in the street and would fill the sidewalks, running past the many High Street businesses just to catch the great spirit of their beloved "Greyhound-Marching-Band." They couldn't get enough of their sound, and they couldn't get their fill of their perfection. It was infectious throughout the city, especially in the "African American" community.

When the Greyhounds of I. C. Norcom took the football field for a halftime show, it was pandemonium in the atmosphere. No one would leave the stadium to go to the concession stand, but they all waited in excited anticipation for the marching Greyhounds' field entrance. The field entrance itself was worth admission. They knew that it was going to be a show stopper from start to finish.

The "drum-major" always took the field first. The band is spread out all around the football field side-line. Once the "drum-major" took the center of the field along the 50-yard line, the show was on. The "drum-major" set the stage right-off, would lean back with his back bent backwards and high-kicking with leaping struts from the sideline in front of the "Press Box" to the center of the football field. When he got to the center, he would twirl the "drum-major's-baton" while leaning all the the way back, backwards until that hat, like the Buckingham Palace guards wear, touched the ground. He would stay there, bent over backwards, for a couple of seconds with the drum majors' baton held up in the air. Then he would give his whistle a couple of tweets and slowly rise, as the band took the field from all points around the field. It was an unstoppable show of marching band perfection and the Norcomites loved it so as to expect nothing less than top performances.

To some extent, drum sections have a certain loyalty to each other. Whereas on other terms, you would have to watch your back as your drum sticks or drum straps might get stolen or "disappear," and no one in the drum section knew anything about their whereabouts.

Tenor drummers played their drums with small mallets and loved to color their white drum hides with colorful art work using an assortment of magic markers.

The Fish Bowl Classic Parade usually took place around the end of September. It was sponsored by the Shriner's of Arabia Temple #12 of Portsmouth, VA. A Norfolk State University football game followed that evening. The Fish Bowl Classic Parade began at the foot of High Street, at the water front. It proceeded up High Street ending at Frank D. Lawrence Stadium. School band directors would receive invitations to have their band participate in marching events. Some of the participants include marching bands from Jacox Junior High and Rufner Junior High in Norfolk, VA, I. C. Norcom, Woodrow Wilson, and Churchland High from Portsmouth, and Booker T. Washington High from Norfolk.

The parade line-up held a special place of recognition for band directors and band members alike. Everyone knew that Norcoms' band would be last in the line-up. They had to be last because they had such a following that as the band proceeded in the parade their fans and following would chase after them to the end of the parade. Once Norcoms' band reached the halfway point of the parade, the number of their following swelled so much that the favorable line-up position would be being the first marching band in the line-up or immediately preceding I. C. Norcoms' band so as to not get caught in the frenzy of their following.

If you lined up as the first band in the parade that sent a signal to the band directors and band members that they were recognized as being a pretty good marching band. If you lined up immediately in front of I. C. Norcoms' band that also told the band directors that their band had an excellent performance rating by the judges and parade organizers.

As we marched with sort of a high-step style of marching, which was somewhat parallel to and even copying the high-stepping style of I. C. Norcom, the drummers were led by a drum captain calling the cadences, selecting particular cadences all along the parade route that created the desired band response and energy level. The majorettes who marched in front of S. H. Clarke Junior High Schools' band were especially fond of the rhythms that came from the drum section.

Former S. H. Clarke Junior High majorette, Everetta "Mickey"

Simmons, who resides in the Portsmouth, VA, area tells me that of all the rhythms that came out of the drum section, she especially enjoyed the cadences that were played entirely on the metal rim of the drum. Mickey expressed that those rhythms on the rim of the drum gave her a sense of peacefulness and tranquility as she galloped and raised her pom-pom clad white cowboy boots to lead the numerous marching band processionals.

The rim cadence occurs when the snare drum player plays the rhythm with the snare sticks on the metal rim of the snare drum. Tenor drummers and bass drummers combine their rhythm on the rim of their perspective instrument or as a soft muffled back beat to accent the bottom of the cadence.

Proper volume is the key. Playing loud has its merit, but bringing the volume down to playing only with the drum stick on the metal rim gives the groove that quiet funk. Once you've played that quiet funk and the listeners have gotten on board with what the drum section is doing, the impact is much more profound when the cadence transitions to a louder funk volume. Playing the entire cadence on the metal rim of the drum is entirely different from the drum beat known as the "rim shot." For the single rim shot, the rim shot is a snare drum beat performed by the snare drummer by playing one snare drum stick, touching the metal rim, laying it lightly across the center of the drum hide and, while holding the drum stick snug to the drum hide, striking that drum stick with a hard quick stroke with the other drum stick to create a shot type sound.

You might not think that cadences struck on the metal rim would be heard throughout the entirety of a moving marching band, but cadences on the rim create that "wow" effect. S. H. Clarke's drummers played cadences on the rim to allow the band to quietly approach and close in on a parade reviewing stand, to allow the band to rest, to continue with the funk in progress, and to bait a rival marching band opponent to think that you're not up to competing against them. On the contrary, cadences on the rim are widely heard by many a parade route observer as responses of affirmation are acknowledged by the drum section, and the band receives high respect as they pass by.

On the parade route, I never knew where my parents would be standing, but I could always pick them out. Their favorite spot to view the parade was on the left side of the street, right at the wall at Trinity Episcopal Church as we approached the corner of High and Court Street, once the band got to the reviewing stand, we were always asked to stop or pass-and-review, playing a march song related to the theme of the parade.

Once that song was finished, the drum section took it upon ourselves to play a real funky cadence as the band moved pass the reviewing stand.

The drum section at S. H. Clarke was notorious for breaking drum hides. There were times when the drum section couldn't finish a band practice or a section practice without one of the drummers breaking a drum hide or even breaking their drum sticks. Beginning with the tenor drummers who beat down on their tenor drums, just above their knee. They thought it a kind of badge of honor to break their hides. Bass drummers and snare drummers followed. Some of the hide breaks were legitimate and happened naturally over time and usage.

The music department provided the new drum hides, but the individual drummer had to learn how to change their own hide. I believe that was one of the driving reasons why band directors started leaning toward purchasing the high-steppers for the drums. With the drum raised off the leg, the drummers could lift their legs higher, and they would decrease the number of drum hides being broken. It also caused the drummer to focus his stroke to upward and outward from the body verses the downward power stroke.

Snare drummers broke their drum hides using the bottom end of the large 3A sticks. As the snare drummer played cadences, eventually it would cause a depression to form on the hide followed by a small slit or cut. Once the slit appeared in that depression, it was only a matter of time before the crease would widen to a larger cut. The drummer would play on that hide until it couldn't be played on anymore which eventually led to replacement. Mr. Mallory got new hides for the drums, and the drummers would go right back out there during the next practice and deliberately start work on breaking that hide.

S. H. Clarke's band formation consisted of a 10-man front; of course the band was comprised of male and female participants. Usually the front 10 were made up of 10 trombone players who always set it off just right with their long valve extension on their horns, for the most part brass instrument players (trumpets, etc.) were male and woodwind or reed players (clarinets) were female except for the saxophones, who were male. There were some clarinet players who would cross over to the saxophone. Flute players were usually female. The percussion section was all male and consisted of 10 drummers. There were four snare drummers, two tenor drummers, two bass drummers, and two cymbal players. One of the favorite and popular marches for drummers and band members alike was "Everything's Coming Up Roses". It was our staple march hymn.

Trumpet players, alto horns, and saxophone players made up the middle of the marching band's formation. Clarinets and flutes were positioned right in front of the drum section. Lastly the tuba or bass horn section lined up just after the drum section making it the last row of the band. The brass on the tubas or bass horns started out as an ugly, dull grey color and then to a sparkling gold color, and later began to change to a dazzling white fiber glass instrument.

I. C. Norcoms' band uniform was maroon and grey S. H. Clarke's band uniform was blue and white complimented with white spats worn over white buckskin shoes. The marching band uniform wasn't complete until the band members had their white gloves on. These were along the line of the type of white gloves that the ushers in the church wore. Some of the players cut the fingers out of their gloves in order to have better access to the keys on clarinets, saxophones, flutes, and valves on brass horns. For the drum section wearing white gloves became a problem. Initially drummers wore their white gloves playing their snare or tenor or bass drum. It was fine for the tenor and bass drum players because they had cowhide strings on the end of their mallets where they could wrap the cowhide around their hands for a tight grip on the mallet handle. The snare drummers had difficulty holding their drum sticks. The sticks would slip out, and the snare drummers just couldn't maintain a sure grip on those sticks. During summer band practice, drummers had already begun to use masking tape to cover the blisters that always came on index fingers and thumbs. Eventually we stopped using those white gloves giving way to taping our fingers and using them only for band uniform inspections during dress rehearsals.

All band practices and band performances were during the daylight hours. City parades were held on Saturday mornings. There was one occasion when we were invited to perform a half-time show for I. C. Norcoms' night football game under the lights at Frank D. Lawrence Stadium. Of course, we, as junior high school students, felt as though we were the top of the heap. It was S. H. Clarke and I. C. Norcoms' marching band set to perform together on the same stage at Frank D. Lawrence Stadium in Portsmouth with no other outside band competition.

S. H. Clarke's band took the field first. With our performance of a seven-minute half-time show, the band exited the field very quickly. I. C. Norcoms' band took the field as S. H. Clarke's band looked on from the stands. Smoke rose from the chalked football field and created an on-field excitement as the Greyhounds high stepped their entrance entering from all points on the field. All routines and musical selections led to their highlight performance of playing the "Norcom Rock." They not only played the "Norcom Rock," but the added dance routine along with the playing from their 50 yard line center position created pandemonium in the stands. Their performance was electric and high on excitement from start to finish. No sheet music was ever used during performance. It was all presented from memory and hard practice. Any band could compete against Norcom, but once they got to their last number, the "Norcom Rock," it was all over. It seemed as though the band covered the entire football field. Their entrance was designed that once the band was positioned on the field, they would be faced right in front of the home stands with an eight-to-five spacing. The stadium rocked. After the "Norcom Rock" was played, it was already a show stopper, but the smoke-filled football field once again took the performance to an even higher level for the on lookers as the band began to exit the field. It was as though the smoke became more heightened and more pronounced when the band started to leave the field. The greyhounds took that field without any fear or trepidation,

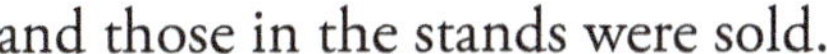

and those in the stands were sold.

Norcom introduced and perfected the high stepping march style and influenced all of the city's high school marching bands. S. H. Clarke had the only junior high school marching band in Portsmouth, Harry Hunt Middle School, a neighbor to Frank D. Lawrence Stadium didn't have a marching band. Later there was W. E. Waters Junior High located in the Cavalier Manor section of the city and Alf J. Mapp Junior High in the Cradock area, but none of those schools had a marching band or any type of band that we were aware of.

The high steps that Norcoms' band instituted were steps where each leg had to be raised to the marcher's waist at a 45-degree angle with the foot pointed downward at an angle. Once it reached that height, the leg was released and lowered to almost a tip-toe touch with the ball of the foot, ending on the ground then quickly snapping back into that 45-degree angle leg raise. Those steps were direct and unwavering, which showed a certain poise in their performance. Actually, that smoke was chalk dust rising from the yard lines of the football field, but when the Greyhound marching band hit those yard lines, it looked like the rising of white smoke. Also the lights from the stadium illuminated the smoke's effect on the performance.

S. H. Clarke's marching band knew that we had no rivals from any of the junior high schools in the area, and we could hold our own with any high school marching band. It was on that large open field just outside of the back door of the band room that we learned to march eight steps to five yards. Once the yardage was measured and marked off with white chalk just as a 50-yard football field, half-time show practice began to take place. We would have practice out there on the field after practicing sheet music in the band room.

The overall sound that a marching band puts out is oh so important. Some bands have weak sounds, and the instrumentation seems to be going in several directions. Marching bands must work at getting a strong sound by the numerous practices that are held in the band room. Band room practice works out the musical bugs of the practiced sheet music. Sheet music is used in the band room practice to learn the music and to get all sections on the same page. That's where the nuts and bolts are worked out. Band sections work at it and work at it. S. H. Clarke's band played with a strong sound. We played with a strong sound like that of a high school band. The brass sections of the trombones and trumpets anchored that strong sound along with the bass horn section.

That's where the drum section comes in to put the icing on that strong sound. When the brass section finishes, it's the drum section's responsibility to pick them up and drive that strong sound home.

Now when the band goes to the practice field everything comes together. The music, the marching between the lines along with incorporating a routine that follows along with certain points in the music score. Various points on the football field should meet with certain parts or places in the music. As band members practice on the field, they begin to see where they are in the formation to where it matches the music. It's the job of the band director to draw all of this up and make it come together by showing his vision to the band. The drum major helps the band director in positioning the band on the field acting as somewhat of a field general.

We never marched with any sheet music in parades or during half-time show presentations. All music was learned in the band room, and we practiced it until we knew it by heart.

At S. H. Clarke the band marched about 50 to 60 members. It consisted of a 10-man front with five to six rows deep, rounding out the total membership. Being a part of the band was valued and respected by all of its participants. The band heightened school spirit and served as the show piece to the public. The public appreciated our involvement in the band.

Snare, tenor, and bass drums were a bright pearl blue in color with crystals in the design.

When I entered S. H. Clarke's band, the band director was Charles Jenkins, Sr. Mr. Jenkins was a strong disciplinarian. He had to be that way for junior high school students who already thought they were grown.

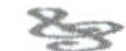

The thing about Mr. Jenkins was that he was a trumpet player. When the trumpet section made a mistake, he would give them his sternest rebuke. As drummers, we were glad that we were not trumpet players or any other brass player.

My second year of being in the band, Mr. Jenkins became Assistant Principal at S. H. Clarke and his band assistant the prior year, Mr. James "Poochie" Mallory took over the helm and became band director. The drum section loved it when Mr. Mallory became band director because he was a drummer. His lead instrument was the drum, and we felt that we were going to get some breaks, perhaps some preferential treatment, and be allowed to just whale out all of the time. That didn't happen, but he made us become more focused on reading percussion sheet music.

After band practices, drummers learned to pull-out from the band and line both sides of the entrance to the band room to allow each section to enter the band room in single file. Sometimes some of the student body hung around at the end of the practice just to see the band march into the band room. This is where the drum section would stay in step or mark time with the rhythm of the cadence and move our right leg in and out with the drum riding on it. It caught on so well that it created its own spirit and lift for the band after band practice. You know that's all we needed as a drum section was that kind of a boost. From then on, after every practice, the drum section prepared to create cadences and rhythms that brought the funk. Rhythms that would hold the interest of the on lookers, and those that would give the band a lift as they entered the band room preparing to depart for home.

Once the band was in the band room most of the instruments were put away in their cases and left on the shelves in the music room. Some of the students took their instruments home for additional practice.

Usually after evening band practices, band members walked home together. There was always some joking going on as we walked. When we took the Turnpike Road route toward home past Norcom High, we stopped off at Jones Grill. Jones Grill was black owned, located across from Jeffery Wilson Homes on Frederick Boulevard. At the halfway point on the route, band members stopped there for a break. We loved listening to the juke box tunes of the day, "Aint Too Proud to Beg" of the Temptations and the Dells' "Still Water." A soda and chips or fries were the usual refreshment. We stayed there for about an hour and then began the next part of our walk home.

Just around the corner on Turnpike Road, Norcoms' band would start their band practice. Band practice for Norcoms' band was an event all by itself. Debbra Jones, a former majorette with S. H. Clarke Junior High and Norcom High explained that the band didn't have a field to practice on. Therefore they had to practice on the front lawn of Norcoms' school building. Well, that made it an event for people to see. Norcoms' front lawn faced Turnpike Road toward Jeffery Wilson Homes. Turnpike Road was a busy thoroughfare of continuous traffic. When the band would begin its practice, they had to exit the band room on the Frederick Boulevard side of the school building and get into marching band formation on the driver's education and school bus pick-up driveway. Once the drummers would crank it up, passersby in their cars slowed up and pulled into the driver's education driveway to get out and see the Greyhounds begin their practice. Cars also pulled to the side of the road, right in front of the school building to catch a glimpse of that Greyhound energy and watch them march from the bus pick-up driveway around the corner of the school building to the front lawn, which became their practice field.

There was an overhead trestle walkway or bridge that went over Interstate 64 which some of us took. It went through the Douglas Park community ending up at the Douglas Park Elementary School, Community Center, and Athletic Complex. Band members used it as a shortcut leading to the neighboring North Truxtun community next door. As we walked each other past their house, I was usually the last to get home since my house was located in south Truxtun.

CHAPTER 11
Times are Changing

In 1967, I began my freshman year at Cradock High School in Portsmouth, VA. The band director at I. C. Norcom High, Mr. Emery Fears expressed interest in having me come to Norcom to be in the Greyhound's marching band. School integration was just beginning in Portsmouth, and I knew that because of the new zoning guidelines that I would be assigned to attend the majority white Cradock High School and become instead a Cradock Admiral. I was honored that Mr. Fears would show interest in my snare drum skills. It let me know that my snare drum skills were alright, that I was respected from the African American side of bandmanship before I crossed over to the "other side." He had interest in taking me to the next level and wanted me to keep it in context with an African American high school experience. Later during band performance outings, I would see him at Foreman Field on Old Dominion University's campus for high school band day competitions and wonder what it would be like to play drums in the Greyhound marching band. Mr. Fears would see me there during those competitions and call me "Cradock!"

Students who lived north of Portsmouth Boulevard were assigned to Norcom High and students who lived south of Portsmouth Boulevard were assigned to Cradock High. I lived south of Portsmouth Boulevard in the Truxtun neighborhood. Therefore, the majority of my band friends lived north of Portsmouth Boulevard and attended Norcom and marched in the Greyhound band. I was the only band member in my class from S. H. Clarke Junior High School that went to Cradock High. Most of the African Americans lived north of Portsmouth Boulevard.

Cradock was basically a majority Caucasian high school located in a white neighborhood. I was surprised when the band first met that there were two African American band members who were members of the drum section, who welcomed me to the drum section, Teddy Greene and Richard

Counsel. They were from the community of Cavalier Manor and were part of the first wave of African American students to desegregate Portsmouth's schools through the school zoning statutes.

Teddy Greene played the snare drum, and Richard Counsel played the tenor drum. The school and that part of the community in Portsmouth, which was called Cradock, had a reputation of being highly prejudice toward African Americans. Teddy Greene became a great help in settling me down on the snare drum and into the drum section, as some of the upper-class white drummers tried to sway me against being true to my style of playing the snare. They tried to influence what I knew about playing the snare drum and take how I played it from me. On one occasion, I remember Teddy telling those upper-class white snare drummers to leave me alone. They backed off, and it allowed me to come into my own as a snare drummer which later served as a springboard to become the section leader.

In those days, most of the school days, we walked to school. The majority of the route went through white neighborhoods all along the way until we got to the school, which was located in the all-white community of Cradock. The first day of school, I wore brown tassel loafers. We knew that the white children loved to wear the tassel loafer shoes and the tassel loafer became the style for African American students. Now, the tassel loafer shoe was a big change for African American students, especially for the male students. It was such a great stretch from the African American male shoe styles of wing tip and biscuit toe Stacy Adams.

Band practice was mostly in the evenings after school, and we would walk home after the practice and walk to school in the mornings. We did a lot of walking in those days. Many white students had their own cars when they turned driving age. During our junior and senior years, some of the African American students also began to drive their parents' cars to school. Sometimes if the band practice ended during the night hours, our parents would pick us up. There were a lot of night practices on the football field for half-time show preparation. All of the half-time shows were performed at night, under the lights.

Such was the climate of African American students at a white

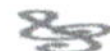

high school, an environment just waiting for something to set things off between the races. All departments in the school were segregated. There were a few blacks on the football and basketball teams. All of the coaches were white until Cornel Gordon came on as an African American substitute teacher in physical education. Cornel Gordon was formerly a cornerback for the New York Jets of the National Football League who had beat the Baltimore Colts in the Super Bowl. He was from Chesapeake, and the students in the gym classes loved to talk to him about that Super Bowl and get him to show them his Super Bowl ring. Later Joe Langston came on as another African American physical education teacher. He also began to help with the junior varsity football players and help as an assistant coach on the varsity football team.

There were no black cheerleaders, and the music that the band played was stuck in an all-white "pop" culture genre. My freshman year, the band played the song called "Dixie," sort of as their theme song. That year we learned to play Dixie, but it did not set well with the African American band members as well as the African American student body. Teddy Greene was adamant, displaying his disdain about playing Dixie as he always tried to disrupt the percussion syncopation and rhythm by speeding up past the tempo and by injecting off beats and rim accents that weren't written in the music, thereby throwing the entire band out of functioning as a cohesive unit.

The band director always tried to find out and catch who was doing it. Whenever the band director walked back to the drum section to see who was doing it, Teddy would straighten up and play it the right way. He never got caught.

In high school, the Band Parents Association played an important role of working behind the scenes on behalf of the band. They were in charge of the concession stands at the football games and actually worked serving half-time refreshments. The band parents were always real nice to the African American band members, especially the parents of the white band members. My father, Milton L. Cox, Sr., became active with the Band Parents Association. I never knew what they discussed at their meetings, but my sophomore year, the band didn't play Dixie anymore. I felt that the Band Parents Association played a part in getting the band to turn from playing Dixie. Also, the band director, Mr. Barley, who was white, wouldn't have allowed that type of spirit to divide the band.

Each year, more and more "African-American" students came to Cradock high bused from their all "African-American" community in Cavalier Manor. Some of the white students didn't want us there, and a lot of the "African-American" students didn't want to be there either.

American students didn't want to be there. Friday was football game day with pep rallies and school spirit day, wearing school colors of maroon and gold. Oftentimes early in the school day on Friday mornings, during home room period, there would appear a straw figure hung from the school clock located on the first floor at the center entrance of the school. It was always a point of conjecture for the African American students especially the African American athletes on the football team. It set the tone of making the statement that "we don't want you to be a part of our school and a part of our school spirit." No one ever owned up to those pranks of divisiveness, but the gesture pointed to some of the white football players. The band became a great vehicle to take hold of the race diversification and interaction among the student body.

Some of the high schools in Portsmouth didn't have their own football stadiums. I. C. Norcom and Woodrow Wilson high schools played their football games at Frank D. Lawrence Stadium. Churchland High School and Cradock High School had their own football stadiums. Churchlands' stadium was on the same grounds as the school building, next to the building, and Cradocks' stadium was on the same grounds as their school building, next to their building.

As drummers, we were always on the brink of starting some sort of beat or rhythm during football games. They tried to keep the drum section quiet during the football game, but to no avail. The band had seats reserved in the stands just below the press box. To get to those seats, the band along with the drum section, created a funk-show all of its own.

There was a wire fence that separated the football field from the track and the stadium seats. The band would march down the front of

the school towards the stadium in the basic band formation and come around behind the visitor's bleachers to the far end zone where there wasn't much light during those night games. We would make it down the track passing fans in our home stands and passing the cheerleaders who were always stationed on the track, which was dusty dirt, in front of the press box. As we moved into place, right in front of the press box where our seats had been roped off, there was a gate that opened leading to the bottom row of bleacher seats which let no more than one person at a time pass through. That gate came up to me just above my waist.

At that gate is where the drum section would take over the scene. The band prepared to pass through the gate in single file. The drummers would exit the formation, march to the front of the band, and form a passage lane with drummers lined up on two sides of the gates' entrance. The band would march through the drummers in single file, through the gate and up to their seats. Of course, the drum cadence for this transition to the stands became ever so funky as the drummers would bob up and down creating a movement that caused the drums to move up and down with the beat. After the band passed through, it was the drummers' turn and you know how percussionists are!

There were times when we would start a little routine on the track before we passed through the gate which set a high spirit with the student body in the stands. We would work it all the way up the stands with percussion funk until we got to our row of seats. It would set it off just right. This didn't happen until my sophomore or junior year. Maybe my junior year, after some of the upper-class white drummers had graduated.

After football games the band began to create its own following as we marched back toward the band room. The march took place in front of the school building where eight large oak trees lined the front sidewalk reaching high above the two story front of the building. Those trees on the left side and the front of the building on the right side created somewhat of a corridor type affect as the band would march on the sidewalk toward the band room. Marching between the school building and those tall trees created its own echo-affect as we got another shot of adrenaline just hearing the drum cadences bounce off of the building. At the band room entrance, the show began all over again as the drum section would pull out of the band, and each section would exit, passing through the drum section, marching up a set of steps and continuing into the band room to complete the performance.

The drum section was the only section in the band that started a "jam-session" routine after football games. The rest of the band would march to the band room and disappear inside the band room. The drum section would always remain outside at the band room door and have a jam-session. Later, the drum major started getting into the act and developed a routine to several cadences. We also moved the jam-session to the bus ramp just around the corner next to the chorus room which was in the music wing next to the band room.

Cradocks' snare, tenor, and bass drums were pearl red in color. Band uniforms were maroon and gold with white gloves. Snare drum hides were tightened so that there was some "play" in that hide to disburse a more rounded sound when struck by the drum stick or drum mallet. Snare drum hides were not tightened "tin-can" tight.

There was somewhat of a competitive spirit among the four high school bands in the city of Portsmouth. All of the African American band members in Cradocks' band knew who I. C. Norcom was, and of its reputation as being "the pride of Portsmouth."

During the marching season, Cradocks' band had gotten into a zone of performing well marching in parades. We were the "intergraded" band, I. C. Norcom was the all African American band. We just wanted to hold our own. The white band members learned of Norcoms' reputation from the African American band members. We also knew that when we were performing in parades or band day competitions at Old Dominion University's Foreman Field or half-time shows at Cradocks' home stadium that we had to step it up a notch when Norcoms' band was there. We weren't that concerned when performing with the bands of the Churchland High School Truckers, the Woodrow Wilson Presidents, or the Western Branch Bruins of Chesapeake, VA. Norcoms' band members always respected Cradocks' band. I didn't feel so bad as not to be attending Norcom. Our school colors were similar. Wilson's was blue and white. Churchlands' was black and orange. Western Branch's was blue and grey, while Norcoms' was maroon and grey.

I was friends with most of Norcoms' band members from our junior high days at S. H. Clarke. Especially Norcoms' drum section. Before the Fish Bowl Parade in Portsmouth, both drum sections would talk and greet each other at the foot of High Street encouraging one another. I was friends with a number of the girls in Norcoms' band. I was friends so much with Norcoms' students that some of them think, to this day, that I graduated from Norcom High School. 1990 was the last year of Cradock High Schools' existence as a school and the last year of a formal class reunion for the African American students who attended Cradock High. Yet I have been invited to several class reunions of I. C. Norcoms' class of 1970 and 1971.

From the start of my freshman year, the composition of the percussion section at Cradock was very different from that of which I was accustomed to in junior high school. I was accustomed to the drum section being all male drummers. In Cradocks' band, there was a white female keyboard (bell) player who carried those bells, and marched with them and played them during the concert band season. By the time I was a senior, there was another white female keyboard (bell) player in the percussion section along with an African American female bell player. Prior to entering my freshman year, I had never really thought about it. Seeing that for the first time made me take notice.

One of the special highlights of my time in the Cradock Admirals' marching band occurred during my senior year, was when my neighbor, Clarence T. Mitchell III better known as "Tommy" entered Cradock as a freshman in the trumpet section. Notables like 1st and 2nd chair trumpet players, David Mancuso and that Baines girl were setting the trumpet section on fire the previous year. These two were white trumpet players. As a freshman, Tommy became one of three African American trumpet players in the section and had a low seating position because of his freshman arrival. Mancuso remained as a senior that year and Baines graduated the previous year. As the trumpet section auditioned for seating positions, Tommy's scores had him positioned to be seated as 2nd chair in the trumpet section, next to 1st chair trumpet player, David Bradley, who also was white. When the results came out some of the other trumpet players directed verbal threats of physical harm toward Tommy, feeling that they deserved to be in that 2nd chair because they had been in the trumpet section a year or two prior to Tommy's arrival. When I saw Tommy's seating position when the band assembled for concert practice, I realized, as I was standing in the drum section, that that was a great leap from the previous year seating and that Tommy wasn't just playing around. He was on his game early on.

When my senior year came around in 1971, a lot of racial tension had been ironed out within the band and the student body. There were African American cheerleaders. The track team had set many records with its majority African American track members, competing in the Southeastern District and winning several district championships during the outdoor and indoor track and field seasons. There was an African American starting quarterback on the football team. The scene had become very multi-racial in its texture.

The school didn't have its own orchestra, and we heard that an orchestra was being formed at Cradock. The orchestra organizer and conductor was Mrs. Jerlene Harding, a female African American orchestra teacher who was the orchestra conductor at S. H. Clarke and Alf J. Mapp junior high schools in Portsmouth. She became the orchestra conductor at Cradock and seemed to float in and out of the school only for orchestra classes.

The orchestra didn't consist of percussion or drum instruments. It consisted of violins, violas, and a number of string instruments. Mrs. Harding requested of Mr. Barley to have some of his band members to play with the orchestra. I became a part of the orchestra as a concert snare drummer. I just transferred over as an orchestra member. A number of other instruments became orchestra members to include clarinets and flutes, oboes and bassoons, saxophones and trumpets, baritone horns and French horns.

Mrs. Harding would drill those string players as if she was a drill sergeant. "One and two and three and four and, one and two and three and four and," she would command them with the wave of her conductor's wand. With her voice, she willed that orchestra music

into the very core of those students' beings. Some of those orchestra notables were Angela Carver, Daphne Waring Sorrell, Michael Eaton, and Ronnie Williams.

Band members were chosen to play in the orchestra based on their ability to sight read sheet music. Mrs. Harding was a go-go-go-go-getter type of person, and we had to know how to read that music somewhat correctly at first sight.

The orchestra flourished under Mrs. Harding's guidance. She moved on to organize and conduct the TAM Orchestra (Tidewater Area Musicians Orchestra) with orchestra members from the myriad of high schools in Portsmouth and vicinity. A TAM Orchestra notable is Woodrow Wilson High violinist, Karen Briggs who has become a very successful violinist showcasing her talents while performing abroad in Greece with international musical composer and director, Yanni. I was not a member of the TAM Orchestra as I had left town and moved on to college.

The majority of the high school bands in the city marched in a stepping style. Norcom was a high steeping marching band. The rest of the bands marched in a stepping style that was close to high stepping, it wasn't so much of an exaggerated high step, but it was a step. The leg actually lifted the foot up off of the ground.

Mr. Emery Fears at Norcom stressed the exaggerated high stepping style, whereas the other band directors didn't put emphasis on the high stepping style. There was no drum and bugle corps type marching by the school bands that we performed with. Norcoms' nickname is the Greyhounds, and it was a "style point" for a Greyhound to step high with quick, precise movements and exaggerate their marching high steps.

The majority of our performances were locally at football games between high schools. Performing in the Christmas Parade, the Homecoming Parade, the Memorial Day Parade, and the Fish Bowl Parade always tended to bring out the best in our performance. During my senior year, Cradocks' marching band was invited to travel to Winchester, VA, to march in the Apple Blossom Parade. The band performed very good and placed well among the other band participants for awards who were from many different points within the state of Virginia.

The Admirals marching band also competed in band day competitions in Williamsburg, VA, at the College of William and Mary and in Norfolk, VA, at Old Dominion University's Foreman Field. Norfolk State University held annual band day competitions there for several years as Foreman Field was used for their home football games. Competition at Foreman Field was exciting in that as a band participant, you had a bird's eye view of all of the bands as they assembled in preparation under super tall stadium bleachers. The different array of colorful band uniforms and percussion sections made it a special scene for those of us in high school marching bands.

High school bands from around the Hampton Roads area, and one or two bands out of the area would participate in the competition. We had enough talented local high school bands to "turn it out" all by ourselves without any help from outside marching bands.

In my freshman year, Norcoms' drum section already had high-steppers on their drums. Cradocks' drum section got them my sophomore year in the band. I was ecstatic about getting those high-steppers. It made carrying the drum easier by getting the drum off of your leg. The high-steppers wear a harness where both of your shoulders went through with an added back- brace supporting the shoulders. The back-brace had crisscross straps. On the front of the harness were two metal hooks that latched onto the drum which had holes on the top of the rim for the hooks to connect to. There was a connection at the bottom rim that had a V-shaped metal bracket with another flat strap that was placed in the stomach area of your waist. Once the V-shaped metal bracket was placed in its connection at the bottom rim, the harness was hooked at the top rim. The drum would have an upward and outward projection in front of your body, off of your legs. As a drummer, you had better balance, and your hands and arms were free and up, which created better arm extension and hand control. With the drum on your leg, as you marched the drum went up and down with each step of your leg. Your hands and drum sticks were always sort of pointing downward because the drum had a natural lean to it as it

rested on your leg. Also with the drum on your leg, it had a tendency to move around on your leg, just above the knee, which was an additional adjustment that you had to maneuver while concentrating on playing the cadence and marching.

When Cradock got those high-steppers, I was more comfortable with carrying and playing the snare drum, and it told me that we were going to be about something positive as a drum section and as a band. When a drum section got high-steppers, it meant that your section was setting higher standards. The high-steppers set the tone for the drum section, and the band had to follow that lead by also setting high standards. With the high- steppers in place the overall outlook of the band began to glow and move toward achieving greater heights as a team of one.

Before the high-steppers, marching with the drum on that one leg was as if you were dragging that leg when you stepped. You couldn't take a full step. With the high-steppers, now we could lift our leg and march naturally like the rest of the band.

For band members, band class was a part of your curriculum schedule. Sections had a band period or block together. The trumpets had their period, the clarinets, the trombones, and bass horns sections, and the drum section. At the beginning, band class was boring, and I would go to sleep in a practice room or lay my head on one of the tables in the back of the band room. Those section classes became a time where we learned the percussion parts to the music that the band would be playing.

It was interesting to sight read percussion parts without the band being there. It was an eerie feeling to have the drum section practice sheet music without the band being there to fill in the gaps in the music. You could use your ear to hear your part. As a snare drummer, you had to read notes and play a particular piece of music with Mr. Barley directing.

After the sight-reading session, the drummers could take a break or practice individually in the practice room. The practice room was where I fine-tuned my percussion skills as a snare drummer. You could practice the sheet music, or most of the time, the snare drummers would get together with the tenor drums and practice the cadences.

In one of the practice rooms, there always was a drum set sitting ready to be played. That's where I got the opportunity to learn how to play the drum set. I could close the door to that practice room and learn how to go around from snare to high tom-tom to low tom-tom to crash cymbal. This practice helped me to move into playing the drum set with the stage band and accompanying several numbers that the concert band featured with the drum set.

1971 began with the selection of the section leader chairs and the band electing officers. I was a senior, and the school atmosphere and environment had changed considerably from what it was when I entered Cradock as a freshman in 1967. The African American student population had increased substantially. The ratio had balanced out with a slight edge to the African American students.

That slight edge was reflective in the band when the first order of business was to elect officers. Someone submitted my name and nominated me to run for band president. I came to band class where the majority of the class were drummers, and Mr. Barley informed me and then the class that I had been nominated to run for band president. It took me by surprise. To me, first to have a drummer run in the nomination was way off center. The president was supposed to come out of one of the "elite" instrument sections, the trumpets or the clarinets or flutes. Not the drum section. This would have never been a consideration in junior high school. Secondly, it was way off center to consider having an African American band member as the president. For sure one of the "in-the-know" white band members would want to press their way to run for the nomination. I couldn't decline as everything was laid out for this to occur. It was a huge step for the band to even consider moving in that direction.

The race was against a white male saxophone player. Even though we were competitors for that office, we were on cordial personal speaking terms before the election. As I began to size up the race, I knew that I had all of the drummer's votes. Beyond that I didn't know how it was going to play out. Those horn sections had a lot of pull and influence and were very cliquish. I really didn't know if I would win over that.

It turned out that I received all of the African American female votes, which won the election for me. There also was a lot of crossover votes from the white band members. I became the first African American band president for the Cradock High School Admirals. In 1971, that was a strong statement as to how race relations and perceptions had changed in a four year period.

In high school, band participation comes in seasons. The first season for band participation is the marching band season. The marching band season accompanies the football team along with the football season. The marching band's initial function is to accompany and travel with the football team. Home games are exceptionally spirited in that it was the drum section and maybe some of the brass section that would set-it-off with cheerleaders and lead high spirited school pep-rallies.

Those pep-rally's took place on Friday morning, the day of the game. It happened down in front of the stage in the school auditorium with the entire student body in attendance. The cheerleaders would lead the cheers to pump up the football players and the student body. The football players loved it because they got to wear their football jerseys all day on Friday before the game and the cheerleaders wore their Admirals cheerleader jacket. The drum section played a key role by adding cadences and percussion rhythms and beats to help accentuate the cheerleaders' cheers. Marching in parades was mixed in with the football season and half-time show performances.

Once the football season is completed, the second season for band participation begins when the marching band transforms into a concert band. The band room always remained set up in concert formation throughout the marching season and on into the actual concert season. The marching band practiced its music seated in concert formation in the band room in sort of a semi-circle formation which widened from the center five or six rows outward.

When concert season begins, that seating formation remains the same. For concert season, additional instruments are added to the percussion section.

This is the season where the drum section actually becomes the percussion section. The name actually changes.

The basic drum section of a snare drum, bass drum, and cymbal remain with the elimination of that single tenor drum. Some of the instruments that are added to the drum section to transform it into the percussion section include the tympani, xylophone, ratchet, calves, cow-bell, chimes, wood- block, triangle and drum set or traps.

Concert band formation maintained a special seating chart that set the tone for inter-sectional competition for seats. It began with the 1st chair, which usually was your top player for that particular section's instrument. Players within that section could always compete, or in the case of Cradocks' band, the band director would choose a certain time during the season to hold chair competitions for that 1st chair player. Usually that 1st chair player became the section leader.

During concert season, bands from the several high schools in your district would form a regional band. My district was the southeastern district. The regional band would be comprised of your best band members of all of the high schools in the district. Participation in this band was based on audition tests reading sight-music. Your band director would recommend who would participate or tryout by taking this test. You were given a copy of a piece of sheet music to practice and prepare for presentation during the audition test and you also had to sight-read and play music that you never saw before. Your participation in this regional band was based on your test score. If you scored below the cut- off mark for the regional concert band, you were assigned a seat in a second concert band called the regional workshop concert band. Each concert band had guest directors from outside of the school district. Band practices were very intense as band members prepared for that ultimate concert performance. We only practiced on weekends beginning on Friday evenings and all day on Saturdays into the late evening. Practices went on for about six weeks leading up to a single concert performance.

In 1970, my junior year, Mr. Barley recommended that I try out

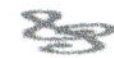

for the regional concert band as a snare drummer. Three or four of the other snare drummers were also recommended. I was the only African American. I didn't make the regional concert band but scored well enough on my sight-reading music to not be disqualified all together as I was selected as 1st chair snare drummer for the regional workshop concert band.

The third season for band participation was the stage band or jazz band. The stage band or jazz band grew right out of the school's concert band and ran in conjunction with the concert band. It was a small set band like the Count Basie band or Duke Ellington style band. This band comprised of four or five saxophones, four or five trombones, and four or five trumpets set up in a small concert band formation with rows set up after the first front row. It took a jazz type turn when it added a piano, a guitar, a string bass, a tuba, and a drum set or traps. The stage band would perform with the school plays and had special event performances of its own on the stage in the school's auditorium. The stage band was selected and directed by Mr. Barley. I wasn't selected to be part of the stage band, but on one occasion I was asked to fill in for their drummer, George Mickley, who wasn't able to make the performance. I also accompanied the mixed chorus with performances on the traps.

My last performance in high school with the Cradock High School Marching Admirals was on Thursday, June 3, 1971, at an 8:00 p.m. performance. The program read, "Swing Out *71, Cradock High School, Concert and Stage bands, William P. Barley, Director."

The concert took place two weeks before graduation. The chairs had been arranged on the football field in concert formation, and the band members practiced to perfection. It was a great idea and setting for a band concert outside in that as darkness fell, the football stadium lights illuminated a final performance for seniors who were a part of change in integrating the school three years prior.

Stage band members were part of the original concert band. About midway of the concert the stage band performed six musical selections. As the stage band performed, the original concert band sat quietly in concert formation, in their seated positions listening to the Stage

Bands' performance. The stage band program of selections were "Big Spender," "Sound of Silence," "Turn Around, Look at Me," "All About the Blues," "We've Only Just Begun," and "Filet of Soul."

The concert really allowed me the opportunity to display my skills as a percussionist, as I played the snare drum and the drum set or traps on six of the nine musical selections presented. I played snare drum on march "Grandioso" by Roland P. Seitz, arranged by Alfred Reed; "Incidental Suite" by Charles T. Smith, which included "Tarantella, Nocturne, and Rondo" and "Chicago" by Robert Lammand and James Pankow, which included, "Wake Up Sunshine," "25 or 6 to 4," and "Make Me Smile." I played the drum set or traps on "3/4 Blues" (a jazz waltz) by Bill Holcombe, "The House of the Rising Sun," arranged by Bill Holcombe, and "Bacharach and David Medley" by Burt Bacharach and Hal David, arranged by John Cacavas. The "Bacharach and David Medley" included "I Say a Little Prayer," "I'll Never Fall in Love Again," "This Guy's in Love with You," "What the World Needs Now," and "Do You Know the Way to San Jose?"

With this performance, the band had achieved a high standard of accomplishment for the Ccradock High School Band.

Autographs of my 1971 senior memories book reads, "To Milton, you are one of the greatest, even though you can't sing. But keep on trying, if you want advice, stick to the drums!!! See you at Big State… Always a buddy, Jo "71" (Jobynia Gary). Marion Harris in the junior class of "72" wrote, "To Milton, I have known you for not quite a year, but I have come to the conclusion that you are a very nice person. I hope you have much success in life…continue to play your drums because you can go!"

Now the 1971 graduation class of Cradock High School sat on the football field for the graduation ceremony dressed in maroon caps and gowns; the class had achieved many milestones with the icing on the cake being Marilyn Gatling, an African American female as class valedictorian for 1971. When my name was called to receive my diploma, I left my seat as our row was standing in line. As I passed around the outside of the several rows of graduates and began to approach the stage, the graduating class began to applaud as I received

a standing ovation en route to receiving my diploma walking across the stage until I returned to my seat.

For the drum section, the difference in the concert season and the marching season was that the drums didn't have to be physically carried by the drummer. During concert season, the snare drum sat on a raised stand where the snare drummer stood behind the drum with their drum sticks extended out, about waist high, reaching the top of the snare drum head. That's where the snare drummer played the snare drum.

The two tom-tom's or tenor drums were mounted on the bass drum while the floor tom-tom sat on raised legs, just to the right of the bass drum.

Usually the smaller 2A size snare drum sticks were used during concert season and a foot pedal with a small mallet connected to it pounded the bass drum. Lastly, the smaller high-hat cymbal stood on its own stand with a foot pedal to raise and lower the top cymbal which sat to the left of the bass drum.

High school marching bands and orchestras had great influence on the African American community. Even in my own neighborhood and on my home street in particular, there were five active musicians with Ronald Washington playing string bass in Norcoms' orchestra, Clarence Mitchell III playing trumpet in Cradocks' band, Broderick Morse playing saxaphone and bassoon in Woodrow Wilson's' band, my brother Stephen Cox playing trumpet in Norcoms' band and myself on the snare drum also at Cradock.

It was so prevalent in the spirit of the youth who watched us doing our thing with our particular instruments that one of our neighbor's son, young William Hayes, about nine or 10 years old, caught the fever early on and could be seen marching down the street into the cull-DE-sac playing on his homemade drum.

Young William Hayes was so taken by the funk and the drumming scene that he made his own drum out of boxes that his father would bring home from the commissary with half-gallons of milk. William tied a string through each side and put the string around his neck with the box as the drum riding out in front of him as he marched up and down the street.

He improvised and got himself some small tree branches for drum sticks and made up his own beats and cadences. On many hot summer days, he could be seen marching tirelessly up and down the street with his drum. William went on in high school to become Cradock Highs' concert band tympani player and marching band drum major.

During my senior year, the drummers were allowed to participate in jam sessions after home football games. Football games were at night, and after the band marched from the football field to the band room entrance the different sections would leave the band formation and enter the band room to complete their night's performance.

From the field to the band room, the band had a huge following, and they all gathered at the door to experience the drummers funk and vibes they could get from the band.

The bus ramp was just off from the band room and after the band had gone into the building the drum section was left outside with the huge crowd beckoning our attention. That bus ramp had a long white overhead roof and space where the drummers could go and take the crowd with them away from the band room door entrance.

Under the bus ramp, the drum section continued the Admirals' spirit by playing a host of cadences and honing our skills. The jam session went on for about 20 to 30 minutes or until Mr. Barley would send for us to come and put our drums up, as he was closing the band room for the evening. We played with no drum section routines it was just the group of us playing our hearts out as we would sit on the steps that led to the chorus room hall and use the closed off entrance as our security to our backs. The gathered crowd had us hymned in up to those doors.

We used those steps so that some of the drummers could take their drums off and give their shoulders a rest. The bass drummers could take their drums off and play them as the drum would rest on the steps. Those of us who were snare drummers kept our drums hooked up. Even though we might have been tired, we sucked it up. The snare

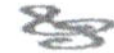

drums played better from the high-step position, so we couldn't put them down on the steps; when the tenor drummers put their drums on the steps, they had to tilt the bottom to keep from getting a muffled sound if they placed the drum hide flat down on the concrete steps.

In the midst of those jam sessions, a popular cadence that was a must rhythm that had to be played was "Wipe-out." It was in the rhythm of the Green Hornet television show's theme song and the surfer's song. The snares loved to work out with that rhythm.

Each year around April, Norcoms' band always got invited to march in the Cherry Blossom Festival Parade in Washington, D.C. It was a whole festival of events in the high profile arena of the nation's capital. Cherry trees were gifts to the district from Japan, and each year, the blossoms were celebrated. As the premier marching band in the Hampton Roads area, Norcom represented the area with all of its fanfare and excellence. I often wondered if we would ever get invited to perform at an event like that, one of those blossom parades.

Well, one year, Cradocks'band got the invitation to march in the Apple Blossom Parade in Winchester, VA, I said to myself that, "Yes, we've got our chance to march in a blossom parade!" I didn't know whether Wilson's or Churchlands' band had been invited to perform in a blossom parade, but Cradocks' band, in some sense, had kept pace with the Greyhounds.

The Apple Blossom Parade was sponsored by the Shenodoah Music Conservatory where our band director, Mr. Barley had attended. He was proud to bring his band back to his school. We enjoyed marching down cobblestone streets nestled in the hilly landscape of Winchester.

Norcoms'only real rival was the Booker T. Washington High School Booker's in Norfolk, VA, another original African American high school. In 1967 and beginning as early as 1965, the students that made Norcom a powerhouse with the new zoning for integration were now starting to attend the remaining predominately white high schools in the city. They were zoned to Woodrow Wilson High, Churchland High, Cradock High, Western Branch High, and later, Manor High.

African American students who attended these white schools viewed

Norcom as their chief rival. It wasn't a rival of hatred but a rival of admiration. It was different in that the African American students who were attending the white schools, in some sense, wanted to emulate the Greyhound's perfection and style.

African American band members in the white marching bands wanted to march in that high-stepping style like Norcom. They would incorporate it in their march style. Soon you would see some of the white band members attempting to march in that style also. Our band directors didn't stress any type of marching-step style; they just wanted us to pick our feet up a reasonable distance off of the ground.

In the city, rivalries were on in every high school focused at Norcom. Athletes wanted to emulate their athletic strength in football, basketball, baseball, and track and field, and possibly beat them at their own game.

CHAPTER III

Jammin' City of Troy

The last week of August in 1971, I began my college career at Virginia State College in Petersburg, VA. The actual site of the school is located in the town just outside of Petersburg called Ettrick, VA. The school was situated on a hill. As you traveled through Petersburg to get to the front entrance of the school, you would pass by the roar of the Appomattox River on your left and make a sharp right turn leading up the steep hillside to reach the circle with a stop light in front of the male dormitories of Williams Hall, Langston Hall, and Seward Hall.

The campus was beautiful in its scenery and calmness. Band members were required to report one week before the student body was to arrive on campus. With a letter in my hand for boarding instructions, meal times in the dining room and a schedule for daily band practices, I became a Virginia State Trojan and had arrived, as Jobynia had mentioned, at "Big State," the school on the hill overlooking the Appomattox River.

I had fallen in love with the self-contained style campus, in awe that this was an African American school. A year prior, my family and I had traveled from Portsmouth to Petersburg to attend the graduation of my cousin, Carl Palmer. The only people on campus for this last week in August were the football team, who had been there a week prior, and the cheerleaders, who arrived a couple of days after the band's arrival.

The weather temperatures in August were always blazing hot as we began daily band practices. Band members dressed for the heat in light colors and hats as band practice never stopped or was never postponed. There were no fainting spells, and no one dared to quit or complain too much about the conditions and no asking for water or water breaks. We worked right through the conditions. The band was known as the Marching 110. We marched about 120 members. The unique thing about the band was that it comprised of music major and non-music major band participants.

When I arrived on the Hill in 1971, the campus was already active in the cultural happenings of the 70s. There was a popular on-campus female/male singing group that performed songs in The Stylistics singing group's genre. Popular hits were "Betcha by Golly Wow" and "You're as Right as Rain." This group set the tone on campus that introduced the 70s funk to incoming freshmen. I sort of felt close to the group of four singers called 3 + 1 because three of the female vocals in the group were from my hometown of Portsmouth. Elton Hawkins was the male group member with Antoinette Saunders, Stephanie Strong, and Brenda Sykes. The terms "home-girl" and "home-boy" or just "homey" became terms of endearment and expressions of closeness.

There also was a campus funk/rock/soul band known as "Trussel," which grew right out of the Marching 110 band comprising of several band members who were music majors, Ron Smith on drums, Hannon Lane on lead guitar, Larry Tynes on trumpet, and Robert Suber on saxophone. Their funk/rock/ soul sound came to prominence with the hit single "Love Injection."

I had arrived at this African American college. During those days, "Historical Black College and University" (HBCU) hadn't been coined, but this is where the happenings were.

The weather was hot, hot, hot, and the school's environment was beginning to heat up for the school year. The school had a reputation of professional excellence. Football players walked around campus guaranteeing victory and giving the new freshman that confidence builder for Trojan loyalty and spirit. They usually came through on their promise. There were professional football candidates as Larry Brooks was called-up to play for the Los Angeles Rams. The Marching 110 itself was already a nationally recognized marching band with Dr. F. Nathaniel "Pops" Gatlin setting the standard at the helm of the music department, and Claiborne Richardson as the director of marching and concert bands.

The 70s, from 1971 to 1973, were a time when it seemed as though a myriad style of music and musical groups flooded the soul/rhythm and blues market and our listening and dancing appetite. From the up-tempo funky grooves to the slow dancing swoon-em-up melodies.

James Brown had already set the tone for the "funk" sound in the 60s as varied new artist's followed: Earth, Wind and Fire; Mandril; the O'Jays; the Delfonics; Parliament Funkadelick; the Tempres; Graham Central Station; the Stylistics; Stevie Wonder; the Dells; Santana; Chicago; Tower of Power; Maze; Heatwave; the Isley Brothers; Joni Mitchell; James Taylor; the Gap Band; K-C and the Sunshine Band; the Staple Singers; Weather Report; the Crusaders; Les McCan; Billy Cobham; the Brothers Johnson; the Emotions; Creative Source; New Birth; the Bar-Kays; Lakeside; Sly and the Family Stone; Archie Bell and the Drells; Rare Earth; the Main Ingredient, Labelle; MFSB (Mother, Father, Sister, Brother); Bobbi Humphrey; Maxayn; D Train; the Intruders; B. T. Express; the Ohio Players; Kool and the Gang; War; the Black Byrds; Donald Byrd; Herbie Hancock; Lonnie Liston Smith; Minnie Riperton; Roy Ayrers; Ronnie Laws; Marvin Gaye; Midnight Star; Brass Construction; Rolls Royce; Barry White; Con Funk Shun; Blue Magic; the Moments (Ray, Goodman & Brown); Sylvia; Brick; Tavares; the S.O.S Band; Starpoint; Rufus with Chaka Khan; Skyy; Slave; Undisputed Truth; the Three Degrees; Evelyn "Champagne" King; Billy Preston; Natalie Cole; George Benson; Love Unlimited Orchestra; Marilyn McCoo and Billy Davis, Jr.; Johnny Mathis; Denise Williams; Norman Conner; Major Harris; Teddy Pendergras; Billy Paul; Gladys Knight and the Pips; the 5 Stair Steps; Dionne Warwick; The Dramatics; The Spinners; Peaches & Herb; Aretha Franklin; G Q; Bobby Womack; Freda Payne; and Atlantic Star.

This is a microcosm of the various array of soulful musical groups that burst on the scene during the decade of the 1970s. These musical groups were the competitors of the Marching 110 and drum section. The sounds they produced created a competition for the Marching 110 to capture the student/audience attention span and keep musical infatuation.

The student/audience was so familiar with those current musical groups and tunes that the Marching 110 had to become more aware and conscious of the music that was out there. The Marching 110s' task was to play and perform a marching routine using the music from that selected soulful genre of funk-bands and maintaining a fresh approach that created excitement and compelled the student/audience to literally sit on the edge of their seats waiting in anticipation for the Marching 110 to step off. These groups echoed the varied rhythms and rhymes that pulled on your heart strings and permeated throughout life on campus. Syncopated down and back-beat rhythms became the backdrop of what it meant to party and have a good time.

Bell bottom pants were the "in" fashion, and the Afro hairstyle was worn by the girls and the guys as a badge of ethnic pride. You would see many guys sitting on the steps of any dormitory getting their hair braided in cornrows by their girlfriends. They would leave the braids in their hair for a couple of days. When they were taken out, the guy or girl would have a large puffy Afro hairstyle.

Now, Petersburg was a drab city. You could say that Petersburg was in a "time-warp." It was a Civil War town where the Union Army tried to tunnel underground en route north to capture the Confederate capital of Richmond, VA. The tunnel caved in which created a huge crater in the city. The Petersburg battlefield is there, located on the street that runs over the crater, called Crater Road. It was as though the city had not grown much since those Civil War days and was stuck in the era of those North-South campaigns.

Richmond was about a 30-minute car ride north of Petersburg. There was a club by the name of "the Mouse Trap" that was the popular night scene of Petersburg natives. For college students, it wasn't an attractive place to hang out, therefore, on the Hill is where we made our own fun. Popular attractions in the city were "the Oak" furniture store and Bradford Manor, a television station with its popular T.V. show "The Bowman Body.

Many days you would find Petersburg High School basketball phenom about to turn professional, Moses Malone, honing his skills around the hoop in the old gym on campus. He was tall and slim at that time and stood above the average VSC student's height. Moses was on campus and in that gym almost every day.

The first day of band practice as a freshman, the entire band came together at 8:00 a.m. in the band room. The band room was located in the music building which was located on front campus beside the president's house overlooking the Appomattox River. The girl's dormitory of Byrd Hall was just across the street from the music building. At this point we met our band director, Claiborne Richardson, Sr., known as "Sticks" or "Stix," and our drum major, Perry "Rusty" Chamblis. The head of the music department, Dr. Gatlin, only stuck his head in the band room and would keep moving.

As our drum major Rusty was a scraping looking, athletic guy, he often wore jean work cover-all's with no shirt showing off the muscles in his arms, and those Omega Psi Phi fraternity horseshoe brands, three in a row vertically over-lapping each other. When Rusty wore those coverall jeans, band members grew to know that we were in for a tough workout at practice.

About an hour after lunch on that first day of practice, the drummers were asked to go outside. Mike Thrift, one of our bass drum players, gestured for us to get our drums and head for outside. That's where it all began, where four new freshmen snare drummers met the current drummers. The four new freshmen drummers were: Robert Kemp and Robert McDonald out of the Newport News and Hampton, VA, area; Ron Smith and myself. I didn't know it at the time, but these four new freshman snare drummers were about to take the drum section by storm. We were percussions on the brink. Edward Thornton and Junious Dyson went outside with us, were already snare drummers in the drum section from the previous years and helped to teach us their already staple cache of cadences and how playing the snare drum was done at Virginia State.

The drum section practiced more by itself on the outside than with the entire band. For the duration of summer band camp practice, the drum section held two outside practices a day, starting early in the morning and breaking for lunch. After lunch the second practice began which culminated with joining the entire band at the end of the day and the dinner hour. The four new snare drummers learned those cadences so fast that it prompted the drum section to start developing and making new cadences. When we started doing that, we began to put our stamp and style of playing on the drum section. The rest of the drummers were impressed with the speed in which we learned those cadences. Robert Kemp, Robert McDonald, and Ron

Smith were music majors. I was the only non-music major of the four snare drummers. My father, Milton L. Cox, Sr., had encouraged me to major in business administration, and that's what I pursued. The snare drummers were the lead drummers within the drum section, and the freshmen music major drummers played their snare drums with confidence and a certain swagger which said that they knew they were good. I knew I had to hold my own with them.

Uniquely, in making and developing new cadences, no sheet music was used. Usually one of the music major drummers would bring the beginnings of a possible new drum cadence and introduce it to the drum section during our outside sessions. Once the cadence was introduced, the entire section had input on adding rhythms or changing syncopations to get that desired funk beat. Even if the cadence began with the rudimental sound, at some point within the cadence, it went to the funk sound. There were some cadences that started with the funk sound and went into the rudimental sound. Some of them started with the rudimental march style, then changed to the funk style and then back to the rudimental sound. We were mixing it up. We were off the chain, and Mr. Richardson let us flow.

I didn't know what was going on when our bass drum players, Mike Thrift and Calvin Powell gestured to us, beckoning us to go outside. I was sure that we were going to continue to practice inside, in the band room with the rest of the band.

The outside area was beside the band room just out of the back door of the music building next to Virginia Hall. There were several Crepe Myrtle trees and a couple of large trees that we used for shade.

From the very onset of my experience in the VSC Marching 110 band, the percussion section operated as an entity unto itself. No other section in the band practiced as an entity unto itself. More was required of the drum section, therefore we had to put more into our sectional practices. We had to clean up all of the rough spots out of our cadences and make them tight and entertaining.

We would work it out and work it out and tweak a cadence for the entirety of a percussion practice and then would bring it back for the

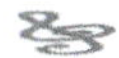

next day's session and tweak it some more until we got it just right. Even after the rest of the band had packed it in for the dinner hour at Jones Dining Hall, you could hear the drum section working it out until everyone knew their part by heart.

All cadences were learned first by ear and secondly by sight. By sight, I mean watching the movement of the drum sticks as a drummer would introduce the cadence, first to the snares, then to the tenor drums and next the bass drummers. There was one or two occasions when the tenor drum and the bass drum rhythms were introduced first, and the snares had to find their groove within their rhythms. Those rhythms made for some funky down and back-beats which inspired the band to take their high-stepping and rhythm control to an additional level of organized movement. It actually energized the band as they stepped off.

By the time that Wednesday of the first week of practice rolled around, the drum section knew three cadences by heart and the percussion sheet music arrangements to two band marches. As we moved toward the Labor Day weekend, the band had to be prepared to put on a half-time show for our opening football game who was always against Norfolk State College in Norfolk, VA. Those football games were always played at Foremen Field on Old Dominion University's campus.

During that first week, the drum section was beginning to gel together as a unit and Edward Thornton decided to leave the drum section and not march for that up-coming marching season of 1971. Also, Junious Dyson kept missing practice or arriving toward the end of practice when we were shutting things down. The section members wondered if Dyson, too, would quit, but he kept showing up. Dyson started to push the envelope for the drum section as he would show up with a cow-bell attached to his snare drum. In practice when marching in formation with the band, Dyson would play that cow-bell more vigorously than he would play his snare drum. We all wondered why he had such an attraction to that cow-bell. By the time we got prepared for the Norfolk State game, Dyson had incorporated that cow-bell as a part of his snare drum ensemble, and we accepted it as we could see that the drum section was headed in another direction outside of the

rudiments and basic march rhythms.

For Mr. Richardson, half-time show performances had to be impeccable and masterfully performed with excitement. He wanted movement from start to finish with crisp precision in that movement.

Each week, our drum major, Perry Chamblis, who went by the name of "Rusty," was instrumental in getting the band pumped-up for a challenge with the opposing school's band. During our weekly practices as the band had gone through a grueling week of preparation, Rusty, on that Thursday or Friday before the Saturday football game, would address the band as we sat in concert formation in the band room. Before that particular last or next to the final practice, before the performance, Mr. Richardson would, very politely, have Rusty talk with the band. Rusty's pep-talk would say that he had gotten a phone call on that day from the opposing school's drum major challenging him in a march-off dual of the drum majors. He would say that he was more than up to the task and prepared to meet the challenge with a performance par excellent. Those statements simmered in the entirety of each section in the band and seemed to be literally speaking directly to the percussion section. We felt that if they challenged the drum major, they were in a sense challenging the drum section. We knew that we had to take it up a notch and be sharp and precise in our rhythms to back Rusty up. Mr. Richardson would follow Rusty's tone setting comments by saying in an upbeat way "Hubba-Hubba band!" "Hubba Hubba Band!", which became sort of our battle cry.

After all, Rusty was the centerpiece, out in front, the first member of the band that an audience would see. Seeing Rusty take the field was totally awesome. You could say, he was energy personified. Rusty was a statuesque young man who willed a type of professional brashness. He had the ability to display finesse and agility with a strong physical presence. As drum major, Rusty would take the field for a half-time show with a burst of energy and precision that let any opposing drum major know and those seated in the stadium that he was the one and that he was in command of this band happening. He would "take" us down the field.

Summer practices lasted all day. The first session started early in the

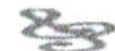

morning in the band room. During this session, the entire band would practice parade march songs and tunes for the half-time show. This session would last until noon, and we would be free for lunch. After lunch, the band would gather in the band room in preparation for the march down to the football stadium. Of course as the band members would exit the band room to begin lining up for marching formation on Hayden Street, the drum section would already be positioned and assembled outside by the street just across from Trinkle and Eggleston Hall as band members would walk out to assemble and stretch down to Byrd Hall.

The football stadium was located two miles on the opposite end of the campus from the music building. The Marching 110 frequently marched the two-mile distance and used the march as a tune-up en route to the football stadium. It became a show of its own as students would bustle along Hayden Street and around down University Avenue to catch the groove as we processed by.

Once the band reached the stadium, the football team would already be there on the field practicing. Band practices were always in conjunction with the football team, both of us on the football field at the same time. The band would work on the south end while the football team would go through drills at the north end and later would leave the field to the band alone. Most of the football team would leave the field as we were arriving. Band members were in awe of the football team as the popular talk about campus was that of the possibility of Larry Brooks, a Trojan defensive lineman being selected to play professional football with the then Los Angeles Rams. He did play and started with the Rams. Band members got a close-up look at his VSC football presence and stature as a football player among his college peers.

Band practices at the football field were geared to move the band toward "perfection." That was where we put the music with the actual band movements on the field. Each note of the half-time show was counted down to an eight step to five yard music score that was most often written by the music majors in the band.

Practice at the football field would last from after lunch until the sun went down in the evening. No matter the weather conditions, practices went on. Normally it was hot weather, but there were times when we would have a heavy summer rain that would mud-soak the football field, including the track that ran around the field. Band practice would go on even in those conditions. It was done that way to condition band members in the event that we were to encounter adverse weather at any performance, we would not quit or stop or better yet lose our professionalism during the performance. If the field was muddy, we would have to perform in the mud. If it was raining, we would have to perform in the rain, without rain coats, in our rain-soaked band uniforms.

After practice at the football field, it was up to the drum section to bring the band back on that two-mile march back to the music building. The fun part of that was that once the student body arrived on campus in early September, they would line the streets and pour out of Jones Dining Hall to check us out as the band made the turn around the corner off of University Avenue on to Hayden Street moving past Virginia Hall and the laundry mat. For the drum section, the brink would be on for funk-based rhythms. Most of the way down from the football field to the music building the band would not play any music and it was up to the drummers to bring it home.

Band members that came to college were considered professional musicians. Therefore, the Marching 110 expected of ourselves to be good at what we did as it was instilled in us by our band director, Mr. Claiborne Richardson. So our attitude as a band was to perform hard, work hard, and be brilliant at it. There was a no-nonsense grit to the Marching 110 band that where ever we traveled in performance, we competed on the highest level and left the names of our competition behind us.

Half-time for college football games were 12 minutes. Therefore, the band had to get on the football field and off in this specified time. The show had to be tight. One that would hold the attention of the fans in the stadium.

Current soul music hits were often played, and we always entered the field through the south end-zone, which set the show off just right.

At about the three-minute mark, the band had to be at the 50-yard line. The Marching 110 used a double time quick step high-step march to get through the south goal posts to the 20-yard line with the entire band on the football field and poised to move toward the 50-yard line.

From the time we left the end-zone until the end of the show, the band had the mindset of being in perpetual motion, non-stop. Once one song was finished, the snare drummers would strike about eight times, and the band would transition into the next song along with the next formation. During the show, the band would stop one time for a concert formation and bring the mood and tempo to a slower groove. VSC was one of the schools if not the first to introduce the "golden girls" to dance, aside from the majorettes, to these slower tempo ballad type songs. These were three girls dressed in glittering gold swimsuit type outfits twirling batons and performing dance routines in front of the band while the band provided music from the top soul tunes of the day.

After the golden girls performed, it was time for the Marching 110 to show off its musical skill. The entire band would perform choreographed dance routines while playing up-tempo musical renditions of the contemporary top chart soul selections of that era. The Marching 110 band at Virginia State College was off the hook. It danced and pranced and wowed the audience between the two 20-yard lines, high-stepping and soulful struts were the Marching 110's signature style of football half-time show performances. Electrifying those in attendance, marching eight steps to five yards, the student body and alumni always remained in the stand staying away from the concession stands and the bathroom to see the Marching 110s' half-time show extravaganza.

As the band exited the field across the VSC football teams' benches, the drum section would take over the atmosphere of the game. From the time that we entered the football stadium, the drum section was always looking for a crack or seam of some sort to start our funktation. There it was as the band was exiting the field. We knew that the band had to rely on us to get from the paved area in front of the seats just below the press box to the section that was reserved for the band. The drum section looked for that break to propel us as percussions on the brink and we took it.

From the time the Marching 110 stepped off of the football field the drum section could not be extinguished from getting on the brink. The drum section knew that it would be in our hands, from the time that the band stepped off of the field until the band returned to the music building. We made it fun and excitingly playful for all of the band members. It took the entire third quarter and into the fourth quarter for the band to re-seat itself in their reserved seating. The drum section played funk beats and rhythms as each section in the band took careful spirited time to return to their seats and rock with the rhythm using their instruments to accentuate the funk of the percussions.

As each section reached their seat, they would remain standing and perform routines with their instruments and hands. This went on until each section found their seating area and the entire band was grooving to the funk.

The last section to return to its seats was the drum section who remained at the bottom of the stands providing rhythms for the rest of the band to get situated. We had to go high-up in the stands, pass the entire band who was standing in their positions grooving to the beat. Once in the bleachers, the drummers sat in the back of the band. We were the last section seated up High Street, just in front of the bass horns. As the drum section hit that first step that led up, the drum captain would call for the cadence to be "African Mumbo." For the "African Mumbo" cadence, the snare drummers would turn their snares off, so their drum would sound like a tom-tom drum. With muffled beats, the snare drummer would step, leaning the snare drum to the side. With the high-stepper to hold the drum the snare drum was very controllable and maneuverable for movement, we would dip and bop and sway that drum up and down and around to whatever effect we desired to the "African Mumbo" rhythm. Each step had the appearance as though we were ascending a ladder. This helped the sound to travel away from us as the bass drummers would back-beat on the snares muffled African-style syncopation. The crowd in the stand would eat it up. They loved it.

When the band got to the stand, the show was just beginning. The drummers never stopped playing, and the band and the golden girls along with the cheerleaders began to coordinate their routines to the drum beat.

During the football games, the drum section kept a continuous funk-beat for the entire game. For the first quarter and the second quarter, the beat provided a sort of prelude for the half-time show. During those quarters, we played a low groove-funk so as not to interrupt the quarterback's signal calling and snapping of the football. All of the drummers kept that low groove-funk except for Robert Kemp. He only knew one way to play, and that was all out. Junius Dyson also collaborated with Kemp's enthusiasm of going all out. The fans loved the low groove-funk. They liked it because they heard the rhythms being played down low, and they couldn't get the full effect of it. It was so infectious that they didn't want that low groove- funk to stop.

At Virginia State, the snare drummer would keep the same snare drum that was selected in their freshman year for the duration of time while in the marching band. It became my snare drum. It was an extension of me when I had it hooked up on me. It had a certain feel and sat just right for my arm extensions. Though all of the snare drums looked alike, there was certain particulars on each drum which made them different. My snare drum didn't have a cow-bell on the side of it. I didn't like that. The cow-bell added more weight to the drum. Each snare drum had a different sound though they were all tightened to the somewhat same tightness, the tightness was different. The degree of tightness made the drum stick bounce off the hide in various heights. I always preferred that my sticks would feel like they went into the drum hide which created a fuller sound when struck which gave it a high lift off of the hide. I also used the same high-stepper for all three years.

Once your snare drum was chosen in your freshman year, it was yours to take care of. It was yours to take care of especially when the hide burst. You were responsible for changing that snare hide, using the drum key to get the busted hide off, and replacing it with a new drum hide tightened to your likeness.

Being in the marching band in college was big fun. Being in the

Marching 110 band at Virginia State College led to the band being considered "legendary" status among the hearts and minds of fellow Trojans and friends.

When the football game was over at home, marching the two-mile distance back to the music building on front-campus proved to be an event of its own merit. As the band would exit the stadium, it had to pass through the back gate that led to the main thoroughfare through campus. Now to get through that back gate was a chore by itself because on game day, that gate entrance after the game would be buzzing with the throngs of students passing through the gate on their way out of the stadium. The back gate would open wide enough for the entire band to march through in parade formation. As the drum major approached the gate leading the band, you could see the crowd divide to let the band pass through. This is where we would pick up football fans to follow the band and walk with the percussion groove all the way up University Avenue. When the band got to the first circle and moved past the student union building, Foster Hall, another show seemed to creep up within the band's emotional gage. Just outside, at Foster Hall, huge numbers of students gathered waiting in heightened anticipation of the band's approach, and it pumped us up even more. When we go to Foster Hall, it seemed as though our high-stepping became more pronounced and higher, and our percussion drive became even the more driven as we were about a third of the way to the music building.

By the time the band had begun to approach the second circle to make that right turn at Jones Dining Hall, the crowds had swollen to numbers too many to count. The drum section would slow the funk down just right so that the band would get the most emphasis in that turn and get it just right. We wanted to make sure that as we slowly turned that corner that the swollen crowd would know that we were there for them to catch our groove and follow us the next quarter of a mile down to the music building. Once we made that turn, we knew that we had captured the crowd. They were coming from every vantage point, out of Langston Hall, out of the dining hall, from behind the dining hall, from behind Virginia Hall, following up from University Avenue and even meeting us as we set it right down Hayden Street. They were coming from the left side of the street and on the right side

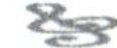

of the street.

After that turn, the band was so pumped up that Mr. Richardson left it up to the band as to whether or not we wanted to play a selection as we marched toward Virginia Hall. Sometimes they wanted to play, and other times they just wanted to groove off of the drum section's rhythms. This is where the drum section began to set the tone for the bands entrance into the music building.

When the band got down to Virginia Hall, another crowd was gathered there, swelling to an even larger size, waiting in anticipation to experience our groove. We would change the cadence up to help refresh the band and up lift their spirits. It also served to get the crowd's attention that something was about to happen, that the band was going to show-down one more time before it reached the music building.

As the band approached the turn into the music building, there was another crowd of waiting students and parents of band members staged at the entrance of the music building for the final groove syncopation and the kick-down. Across the street, students poured from the alleyways between the girls' dormitories of Byrd and Trinkle halls.

The band would make that left turn just in front of the music building, and Rusty would hold us right there. We would march in time, lifting that one left leg on the one- and three-beat, just enough to keep the groove going. The drum section would exit the band and form two lines in front of the band that led up to the steps that went into the band room. The two lines were formed in that there was a passageway in the middle, sort of like the soul train line. Rusty would signal with whistle tweets for each section to exit the band and pass through the drum section passageway on into the band room.

The bass horn section was always the last section to pass through the drum section passageway and on into the music building. When they were in the building, Rusty would give whistle tweets for the bands kick-down. The drum section would be the only section that Rusty gave the kick-down to, which ended all marching band activity. It was called and verbally shouted out "kick-down-VSC." Once the drum section performed kick- down-VSC, it marked the end of the bands day of performance. The drum section would go in the music building and crowds of students would remain on the outside, just hanging out enjoying what had transpired.

One of the home football games, the drum section, in noticing that the crowds would not leave when the band had finished and had gone inside of the music building, saw another seam or crack for percussions on the brink. It was a call for an encore, beyond-kick-down-VSC.

Virginia State's Marching 110 band was a natural high-stepping band versus an exaggerated high-stepping band. It was a normal lift of the marching step where the leg lift had to be at a 45-degree angle with toes pointed down toward the ground. Mr. Richardson knew that as an African American band, we had to be better than good, marching in a style other than that would be slow in effect. We were looking for not a military stoic type style, but a fun and liberating style with precision that was infectious and fun for onlookers. It had a great effect on polishing the sharpness of the bands style.

CHAPTER IV

Beyond Kick-Down VSC

None of us band members knew that there was a whole other untapped avenue of entertainment venue just sitting there waiting for us to open its door and go through it.

Sometimes high school band directors would try to keep the lid on this kind of untapped entertainment avenue, feeling that it would take away from the discipline and performance of the band. Mr. Claiborne Richardson saw that in the third and fourth quarters of home football games that lid was starting to come off. At the music building entrance, he encouraged the drummers to push the envelope and allowed us to return just outside at the music building entrance and give a percussion only performance where band members started coming out of the band room to catch a glimpse of what was going on.

The drum section discovered this avenue after one of our home football games. After Rusty had given the kick-down and the band had gone into the music building, the bass drum players noticed the crowd still hanging outside of the music building. It was a crowd that surpassed the usual crowd of waiting band parents and friends of which my own parents, Mr. and Mrs. Milton L. Cox, Sr., were some of those that would remain.

I had taken my snare drum off and was about to go into the music building to put my drum up when I heard the bass drummers calling for, I thought, the band to do something, but no, they were calling for the drummers to come back outside.

During summer practices, the freshman drummers were introduced to a new cadence called the "toilet stool." "Toilet-Stool" was a cadence where the snare drummers would jump into a seated position, as if being seated on a toilet stool, with their snare drums out in front held by the high-stepper drum straps and brace. The snare drummer would take choppy little steps while playing in that seated position that led to a snare drum dip to the right side playing a single stroke and moving forward through the drumline like that of the soul train line.

During football games, the drum section would never use the toilet stool cadence. Here was a chance to use this cadence that had never been heard before by bystanders or the routine that went along with it never seen. When the drum section got back outside and were assembled, the drum captain called out loud, "Toilet-Stool Position!" When that call came out, the drummers hustled and bustled, bumping into each other. The bass drummers and tenor drummers formed two lines with the snare drummers at one end poised and ready, seated in that toilet stool position balancing ourselves with knees bent in a stoop-down position. Snare drum sticks were out in front hovering over the drum hide.

The next loud call out by the drum captain was, "Hit it!" and the percussion drumline was officially born. For bragging rights, the VSC Marching 110 drum section from 1971 to 1973 were the pioneers of the drumline.

With choppy little steps, in a stooped position, one by one each snare drummer moved through the line, inching forward toward the cadence finish with two snare drum dips, and the routine repeated itself.

As the playing began you could see band members running out of the music building coming outside to see what was going on. Some of them were still in uniform and others were already in street clothes. The drum section never took any part of their uniform off during band performances. We always performed in full uniform, even after kick-down-VSC.

After the toilet stool cadence the drumline would go into the "African Mumbo" cadence. During the 70s, the "African Mumbo" cadence took the drum section to the top of its percussion genre. It was a cadence that connected with our culture which took very well with the student body of the 1970s.

The drum section could have just stood outside in front of the music building, going through a cache of cadences with no body movement. The bass drummers wanted to put some action and movement with

the cadences. It was very entertaining for the crowd, and it served also to boost our energy. After the "Toilet-Stool" and "African Mumbo" cadences, we would go into several other rhythms to round out the performance. The drum section performed and jammed more after kick-down-VSC. There was no time limit on beyond kick-down-VSC.

During homecoming, the crowds swelled so tremendously that we had to move the drumline jam section from the music building to the grassy area between the music building and Virginia Hall on front-campus. Alumni and friends filled that area on front-campus to enjoy the rhythms and sounds of the VSC drumline. My parents, Mr. and Mrs. Milton L. Cox, Sr., usually came up for homecoming and would witness the drummers jam session after the game. Some pictures were taken as this was the era just before the video camera became widely used. I took pictures for my parents after the performance, on the steps of the music building on front-campus with several members of the drumline, along with other band members and some golden girls.

Practices on that Monday after a game performance served as a time to fine-tune our cadences. Routines were added to each cadence as we would prepare ourselves for the next band outing. We incorporated a touch of excitement and expectation in those upcoming drumline performances. Beyond kick-down VSC for the next home football game performance pulled some unexpected surprises for those of us in the drumline.

When the band made that slow left turn just in front of the music building, Rusty whistled for the drummers to exit the band to form its line so the band could pass through them and enter into the music building. As the drum section got into position just in front of the steps to the music building entrance, we noticed that the trumpet section was marching around in circles on the outskirts of the entrance. Then we looked again and the saxophones were marching around in a circle and the bass horns also had quartered off an area and were marching around in a circle.

When the remainder of the band had gone inside of the building, Rusty gave whistle tweets for the trumpet section to pass through the drumline on into the music building. The trumpet section didn't just simply pass through the drumline, but it started cutting up and putting on a show with a choreographed fun-spirited routine that took all of the drummers by surprise. As they approached the drumline entrance, Rusty gave more whistle tweets for the saxophones to pass through, and they began their own fun-spirited choreographed routine which captured the excitement of all who witnessed it. Next the bass horns broke out into their own choreographed routine with additional whistle tweets from Rusty. Before the drum section could break down for its drumline jam session, other sections in the band had caught fire and put on their own jam sessions.

"Beyond kick-down-VSC was born and took on a life of its own. It set the tone for band performances. Band members couldn't wait to get back to the music building to set it off. It energized all aspects of the bands' performance. You would see other sections of the band out on front-campus developing their own choreographed routine after band practice and even before band practice.

The African American genre of marching bands are vastly unique and different in that they are under-girded and woven by the syncopated rhythms of African antiquity. When cadences were being created by the musicians in the percussion section, the rhythms may initially begin with carefully constructed rudimental beats but would move to what one might call African-funk or bounce. It's the funk or bounce of a rhythm that becomes infectious and then easy and fun as it flows through the band. The band catches the infection and movements become very demonstrative. It, therefore, becomes very important for the cadence to have that bounce or funk.

"Beyond kick-down VSC allowed band members in the Marching 110 to break out of the normalcy of marching band performances. It pushed the envelope that all began with the drum section always looking for avenues to go on the brink. In beyond kick-down VSC, the drum section used it as an opportunity to spotlight the individual skills of each drummer while remaining a cohesive unit. The four snare drummers that started out as freshman remained together for three years as Marching 110 percussionist.

Robert Kemp played his snare drum with a type of reckless

abandon. When he played and really felt the groove, you could see his head bobbing up and down. His stick-action on the snare drum became controlled- wildness and infectious to the other snare drummers. It was so strong of an affect that the other snare drummers were pulled in to his exuberance. Kemp was always "on the brink," all by himself. You could see it in his eyes; if we didn't want to come with him on that brink, he would go out there all by himself.

Kemp was flashier than the rest of us snare drummers. He loved to twirl his snare drum sticks through his fingers while continuing to play any funk groove cadence. Just the sheer joy of knowing that he was good saturated all of his energy. In some sense, Kemp loved to put it in your face that he was good. His stick twirling was an acknowledgment of him just out right having a good time while fellow snare drummers saw it to some degree as showboating. If you let him pull you in, you'd lose your center. Once he got those quads, he could combine the stick twirling and showboating to add the desired flare to the drum section's beyond-kick-down-VSC performance.

Our second year in the percussion section, the quads were introduced. It was as though somebody had made those quad drums especially for Robert Kemp. The quad drum was four tenor drums of four different sizes and tones that were reachable with snare drum sticks around a semi-circle in front of the drummer. The drummer could march with them, braced on, from the shoulders. That year, Kemp left his snare drum and took those quads on a journey. I don't believe they could have envisioned what could have happened to them. In playing those quads, Kemp put the drum section on the cutting edge of percussion innovation.

All of those freshman music-major drummers played their snare drums with confidence and had a certain swagger about them.

Robert McDonald was the more rudimentally sound of the four snare drummers. You could hear all of his accents and every stroke in his open or closed rolls. Mac played with strong balance in both his left and right hand. Quiet and cool, Mac also could take you on the brink all by himself.

Once he got that smooth groove stroke of his going, he would holla at me and say, "Milton, come on, let's go!" When he would say that, I knew that he had connected to some type of drum adrenaline and was in his element.

Ron Smith was cool in his demeanor. He wore mod clothes, knitted skull caps, and rawhide vests with tassels. He had a pouch hanging down on the side from his belt that also had tassels. Ron even talked in a that cool funk type lingo. Ron was soulful and "down-with-it." You just knew that his drumming was ingrained within him. He never got flustered, and for him it was all about the groove. Ron played his single snare drum as if it was a drum set.

Some of the marching band's music majors started a campus funk band known as Trussell, and Ron branched out with them as their drummer on the "Drum-Set". Just Ron's presence and demeanor told you that he was already "On-The-Brink" before the "Brink" ever got started. It didn't take much to take him there. It only took a flicker, and Ron was already there.

Of the four freshman snare drummers, I was the only non-music major. I always played my snare drum with a wrist-action that created "high-stick-action." Once my sticks hit the "Drum-Hide," they were always being lifted up off of that hide, which kept my sticks in the air. The brace on the "high-stepper" helped my posture as it straightened my back and my head was always held up at a position of being out in front, on point, for getting on the brink.

There was no intersectional challenges of one-upmanship or competitions. We all respected each other's gifts, talents, and style. We meshed together as one unit and learned to add additional skill to our individual talent from the other drummers.

My second year as a member of the Marching 110 was Rusty's senior year and last year as the Marching 110s' drum major. That year Kevin Curtis (from Richmond) had been the captain of the "Drum-Section." The next year, Kevin took over as "Drum-Major" a s he had experience as the "Drum-Major" at Magie Walker High School in Richmond, Virginia.

During that, my third year summer band camp practice, Kevin took over as "Drum-Major." There was talk going around within the section as to who would be the next captain of the drum section. The "Drum-Section" practiced all through "Summer-Band-Camp" without a "Drum-Captain." Without a drum captain, it was a matter of which drummer would make a decision on calling the cadences. I stayed out of the fray as bass, snare, and tenor drummers alike took turns jockeying to call their favorite cadence.

Toward the end of our summer band camp practices, the band had lined up in the street in marching formation when Kevin came from the front of the band, walking through the sectional ranks, stopping to talk with the drummers. He came over to me and was talking band talk between a couple of us, and to my surprise said that I would be the next captain of the "Drum-Section." I was astonished to be selected as the "Drum-Captain" because I was not a Music-Major. I was so sure that one of the music major drummers would be selected. Kevin told me that I knew all of the cadences.

Some of the cadences were called by lifting up drum stick symbols in the air. Some were called by hand symbols and verbally calling out a particular cadence name. I began my third year in the Marching 110 band as "Captain-Of-The-Drum-Section" in August of 1973. The"Drum-Section" rallied around me as we didn't miss a beat in our being a solid unit.

The "Captain-Of-The-Drum-Section" was responsible for "Cadence-Selection." "Cadence-Selection" was based on where the band was during the parade route, the location of the onlooking crowd on the parade route, and the emotions and energy level of the band. the "Drum-Section" just didn't like the "Cadence" that had been called or There were times when a certain cadence didn't work for where the band was emotionally. Sometimes the drum section just didn't like the cadence that had been called or signaled for, and that "Cadence" was changed immediately by the "Drum-Captain."

Virginia State has one of those dug-out-of-the-earth type football stadiums. Rogers Stadium was somewhat in keeping with the hilly and crater type scenery of the Petersburg area. The atmosphere of the stadium lends itself to "Marching-Band-On-The-Brinkness."

In Rogers Stadium, not only did the "Drum-section" feel the urge to be "On-The-Brink", but during football games, "On-The-Brinkness" would catch fire with the entire band and the "VSC Cheerleaders" as well.

At times, the cheerleaders would stand there and gaze at the "brinkness" of the band. After they got their gaze on, they found a way to start their own "On-The-Brink". It was under the direction of Dr. Katherine H. Bennett that the "VSC-Cheerleaders" began their "On-The-Brink" routines.

Whenever the drums would crank it up, the cheerleaders jumped right in, which helped to encourage our efforts as a "Drum-Section." I called them "The-Hardest-Working-Cheerleaders-In-The-CIAA-And-Beyond." The cheerleaders became as much a part of Rogers Stadium "On-The-Brinkness" as the band or the "Drum-Section."

CHAPTER V
Traveling to Legendary Status

All marching bands have reputations and all marching bands have a following. When the "VSC-Marching-110-Band" came out of those summer band camp practices, we were already "a good" college band. For opening day football game half-time shows, the band always began in rare form. "Drumline" performances during "Kick-Down-VSC" helped the VSC marching band become a great college band destined to become legendary in the marching band rankings.

It was the traveling that changed the VSC Marching 110 band's reputation from a great marching band to a legendary marching band. Traveling to away football games and performing on away college campuses excited Marching 110 band members. Traveling and performing away from "the Hill" sharpened band members' drive toward perfection. Musicianship, showmanship, skill, and discipline were all challenged when the marching band traveled. We always wanted to be our best and desired to raise the bar each time we performed. It was sheer excitement for the band to travel as the Trojans' highest desire was to return to "the Hill" as conquering "hereoes & sheroes."

The band even had a good following at opposing schools. The opposing schools' student body usually offered favorable responses to our performances and cheered our way. It was the opposing schools' marching bands that tried to distance themselves. Popular historical black college and universities (HBCUs) away schools included Howard University in Washington, D.C.; Hampton Institute in Hampton, VA; Elizabeth City State College in Elizabeth City, NC; Saint Paul's College in Lawrenceville, VA; Delaware State College in Dover, DE; Virginia Union University in Richmond, VA; and Norfolk State College in Norfolk, VA.

There was a guy on campus who everyone knew, and he knew everyone. "Tidewater Slim" was already a legend on "the Hill." "Tidewater had no classes to go to and didn't live in any of the male dormitories. None of the students knew where he lived. He would just show up and help with the band and athletic teams and love to hang out in "the Grill" in the basement of the "Student-Union" building om "Foster Hall." "The Grill" was where you could get a hamburger and fries and their "famous-cheese-sandwich" along with 3.2 beer.

The unique thing about "Tidewater" was that he had the knack of knowing something about you before you even arrived on campus. He knew what Hampton Roads city you were from, what high school you came from, and he knew something about your family.

No one ever saw "Tidewater" leave campus to go home. He had no car and walked everywhere he went. He would just disappear. He was a campus fixture. "Tidewater" was tall and slim. Talk on campus was that he might be some kind of warlock.

For away football games, the band would leave campus on buses with "Tidewater" standing there watching us depart. Often he would help us pack the buses for travel. When the buses pulled on to the away school's campus, "Tidewater" was already there to greet us as we got off the busses and would help the band unpack. In the meantime, "Tidewater" had already gone around the away school's football stadium and campus bragging on our anticipated arrival. When band members got notification of this bravado from "Tidewater", we knew that we couldn't let him down, "Tidewater" was one catalyst to help boost our reputation to legendary status.

There was no official "battle of the bands" or individual sections from opposing bands competing against each other. Though that spirit was already there, there was no up-close face-to-face sectional competitions. Marching bands sort of competed in those days during football games by musically out toning and out sounding the opposing band across the football field while remaining in one anothers stadium seats. If you couldn't hear the tone quality of the other band from across the football field during time outs while the game was in progress, you would say that your band "beat" the other band.

If the other band had poor tone quality or the songs were unrecognizable, you could claim the bragging rights to beating the other band…or we high stepped higher than the other band…or we were more ferocious in our marching style than the other band…or the audience was more captivated by our performance than the other band and gave one a standing ovation over the other…or one band received louder hoot-calls from the audience when exiting the football field after the halftime show performance.

Some of the opposing schools didn't have marching bands, but they were always very much appreciative of the Marching 110s' arrival on their campus and performing halftime shows in their stadiums.

There were times when the traveling to away football games when the opposing school's band just didn't want any parts of the Marching 110. On several away football games, "Drum-Section" challenges after the football game tried to take hold at Howard University in Washington, D.C., and Hampton Institute in Hampton, VA.

For instance, on an overcast, cloudy day, after the football game, the "Marching 110" remained in the stands playing several popular songs. Sometimes at away stadiums after the football game, the band would remain in the stands and play songs that the opposing band would respond to playing songs of their own rendition. After we played a couple of songs, we noticed that the stadium and the whole athletic area had cleared out. Howard's band had left the stadium and had gone in their band room. Apparently, their band room was just off from their football stadium. Some of our band members, especially our drummers, ran behind them and tried to retrieve their band members back to a stadium "Show-Down", to no avail. With their "Drum-Section" being the last to go into their band room, our "Drum-Section" gpt the message tha they didn't want to be challenged. We left it like that, left D.C., and returned to "the Hill", unchallenged as conquering victors.

Whether it was a home game or away, the football game with Hampton Institute of Hampton, VA, was always the last football game on the Trojans' football schedule. For this game, the clouds burst as there was a huge down pour of rain that filled the track around the field at Hampton with a pool of standing water. In order to get to our seats in Hampton's football stadium on that day, the Marching 110 band, with rain-soaked band uniforms, marched in a pool of standing water on the track. We took our seats in the stands and brought "the Brink" with us. Hampton's band was there also along with the Marching 110, and for the entire football game, the bands battled across the football field with each band playing their own style of soulful hits. In order to keep from thinking about being soaked with rain, as it continued to rain for the entire football game, we went at one another from the time we got off of that wet track, through each band's half-time show, to the end of the third and fourth quarters of the football game.

Though our uniforms were soaked, the rain wasn't a deterrent. The rain and not being able to get out of the weather set off a spirit of competitiveness that deep down the Marching 110 had been waiting for something like that to jump off between other schools.

None of those school's marching bands or drum sections wanted to challenge the Marching 110. Not Norfolk State or Delaware State. Not even Morgan State College out of Baltimore, MD. Saint Paul's College, Elizabeth City State, and Virginia Union didn't have school marching bands, and Howard's marching band just didn't want any part of the Marching 110.

Playing and performing on a rain-soaked football field and in the wet stands for the entire football game, battling back and forth, you would think that by the end of the football game the band members would be exhausted. We were, and we were ready to change into some dry clothes, but while we were still in those wet uniforms, something happened that changed how 'African American' marching bands and especially how how 'African American' "Drum-Sections" hold fast and take to to heart the marching band experience to make it a uniquely creative form of musical expression. Nobody does the marching band experience like the sons and daughters of the "African Diaspora."

After the football game on that rain soaked day, both bands left the football field marching towards Hampton's round-shaped white-stucco, music building. Hampton's band got to the music building first, and the Marching 110 arrived shortly after. When we got there, Hampton's band had kicked down and were going inside of the music building. The last section outside was Hampton's "Drum-Section". As soon as the Marching 110 "Kicked-Down" the "Drum-Section moved" out of the ranks and hurried toward Hampton's "Drum-Section." As the "Drum-Section" was about to go into the music building. I led the

Marching 110"Drum-Section" in asking Hampton's" Drum-Section" to stay outside and have a "Jam-Session." I grabbed one of Hampton's "Tenor-Drums", turning the drummer around to face our "Drum-Section", and as I was asking, our entire "Drum-Section" beckoned Hampton to stay outside to have a "Jam-Session-Challenge" with us.

To our surprise, it stopped raining, and the sun came out as "Beyond-Kick-Down-VSC" and "Percussions-On-The-Brink" came together when the "Drum-Section" of the "Pirates" of "Hampton Institute" battled the "Drum-Section" of the "Trojans" of "Virginia State College's "Marching 110 Band" for about an hour and a half on Hampton Institute's campus in front of Hampton's music building. Our drummers were happy that Hampton's "Drum-Section" stayed. As each "Drum-Section" took turns to start their beloved "Cadences," we notice that Hampton's trumpets and saxophone players had wandered back outside to perform routines to the rhythms, and some of the "Marching 110" members joined in the fun. There was no winner or loser to speak of, but it was a happening, the beginning of the 1st "Batle-Of-The-Drumlines" which took place in "Circa, October 1973".

As previously mentioned, traveling can make or break a band's reputation. It can improve its reputation or it can detract from its reputation. During the football season, the Marching110 had a busy performance schedule with home and away games. Every weekend, the band had performance destinations to prepare for. Even when the band didn't have a weekend to perform in support of the football team, Mr. Richardson would plug in performance dates on the football team's bye weekend or where the away school was less competition for the football team or a school didn't have a marching band.

On this weekend, the football team had a bye weekend, and the "Marching 110" was scheduled to travel for a performance. The buses were packed with instruments and band members. As the buses were leaving campus with approximately "110 Marching Band Members", "Majorettes", "Golden Girls", and "Tidewater Slim" on board, I gazed out of the window. As I gazed out of the window, I saw a poster tacked up on the board at the corner of Hayden Street and University Avenue that read, "The Delfonics to perform at Daniel Gym on Saturday night." I was so disappointed that I was leaving campus that Friday evening and wouldn't be able to see one of my favorite musical groups known as the Delfonics. After missing that concert, I vowed that the next time I was anywhere close and knew that the Delfonics would be performing or coming to town that I would make it see them by hook or crook.

Now, missing the Delfonics was one thing, but the other thing was that the buses were en route to New York City to take the "Marching-110-Band" to perform a "Half-Time" show at Yankee Stadium in the Bronx. Yankee Stadium: the house that Ruth built. We were scheduled to perform this half-time show during the football game between the then Baltimore Colts versus the New York Giants of the National Football League.

Early on, during summer band camp practice, the "Marching-110-Band" was made aware the we had been invited to perform this "Half-Time" show, and all of our performances leading up to this were geared to raise our level in preparation. When the "Marching-110-Band" got to New York, we were ready. Our confidence was riding high as we knew that the half-time show would be viewed by a televised audience, and the "Marching-110" would receive national exposure for the school on "the Hill."

The weather was overcast as we arrived in New York City. The band had housing arrangements at the YMCA while the instruments remained packed on the buses; coed male and female band members were roomed separately. Saturday night, it was party-time at the YMCA, but on Sunday morning, the "Marching-110" awoke poised to take "the Hill" and extend its reputation on a national stage.

The gate to "Yankee Stadium's" south entrance was in the neighborhood just off of the street. The buses pulled up right next to the stadium gate. It was a gate not like entering in a building and closing the door behind you, but when we passed through that gate, we were still outside of the stadium. It was like a double wide gate. The "Marching-110" unloaded their instruments on the sidewalk between the buses and the stadium gate. Walking just a few steps through that gate, we were inside Yankee Stadium. Once we were inside, the stadium didn't seem large at all.

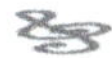

The band had gathered in the grassy grove area just on the other side of the gate we had just entered through. Now our backs were facing the bars of that gate, which extended upward making sort of an arch at the top, as we gathered our directional bearings to stage our positions to enter the football field. Rusty was showing each section where their positions were for our entrance during half-time.

Just then, the sun broke out as we assembled in that grassy grove area. When the"Drum-Section" walked by to get into formation, we noticed the "Bass-Horn-Section" standing with their backs facing the bars of that gate with a sort of stance or "attitude" that we hadn't seen before of them.

At "Yankee Stadium" in New York City, the "Bass-Horn" players had caught the fever and showed their form of "Being-On-The-Brink." The 10 ivory fiberglass bass horn players lined up at the grassy grove area before the band could organize and before the drummers could get into place. They stood, five on one side of the gate entrance and five on the other side, with "Dark Sun Glasses" covering their eyes, with the "Bells" of their "Fiberglass-Bass-Horns" riding downward, toward the ground. None of them would flinch or crack a smile. The "Drum-Section" knew that their light had been turned on and that they would be there to support us and match our "On-The-Brink" performance, which everway the rhythms went. We knew that they would be there for the rest of the marching season.

When the "Marching-110" took the football field, it was as though the band had been swallowed up into this huge valley of a gulf with towering seated walls surrounding us. We had arrived on the national scene, and this was the house that Babe Ruth built.

The "Marching-110" had it's own "Half-Time" show announcer who had the ability to set the tone for a Trojan half-time show extraordinaire. The field entrance at Yankee Stadium was shear perfection.

Rusty took the field first, galloping from the south end zone goal posts, moving between the "Drummers" to the center of the field at the 30-yard line. After his own personal "Drum-Major-Entrance-Show, with one long whistle tweet and four short tweets, the "Marching-110" stepped onto the field coming from five directional points at the "South End" of the field and into "Legendary-Satus." The entrance by itself was meant to be a show of its own as the band used a double-time high stepping style field entrance that took only seconds for the entire band to get on the field. At the 20-yard line back to the end of the end zone, the drum section stepped off right under the south end zone's goal post and used those posts to center its entrance and march right up field. The rest of the band used the "Drum-Section's" position under the "Goal Posts" to "Center" themselves as they got to their prospective yard lines.

With blazing blue band uniforms that matched the blue of the New York Giants' football helmets, the "Marching 110" performed it's "Half-Time-Show" routiene marvelously. It upheld their reputatuion of being a precision-driven, seven-minute machine-like performer which expanded as a move toward "Legendary-Status."

It was only my Freshman year in the "Marching-110-Band", and we were on the cusp of national recognition among "African American" college marching bands and could and would hold our own with any college band in the country. The "Marching-110-Band" of Virginia State College in Pertsburg, Va, returned to "the Hill" as victors and a great sense of accomplishment.

The second year that I was a member of the "Drum-Section" in the"Marching-110-Band " beginning in the "Summer of 1972." The disappointment of summer band camp practice was that the band was informed that it had not been invited back for a return half-time performance in New York City (the Big Apple) at Yankee Stadium. Returning band members felt a big letdown. The question is how do you top having performed a half-time show at Yankee Stadium. Mr. Richardson turned the band's emotions and spirits around as he announced that outside of our home and away engagements the band had been invited to perform a half-time show in Philadelphia at Veterans Stadium. The football game would be between the Washington Redskins and the Philadelphia Eagles. Also that year, we were slated to perform in the "African Ameican, Ujima Football Classic" in Hartford, Conneticut between our "Virginia State Trojans" Verses the "Deleware

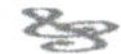

State Hornets."

Veterans Stadium in Philadelphia had just opened in 1971. It was all the rage in the National Football League as the home for the Eagles.

It was also all the rage because it was one of the first football stadiums to use the new form of surface on the field called "AstroTurf." The AstroTurf was a carpet-like surface on the football field that gained popularity from its initial installation at the Astro Dome in Houston, TX. It took the place of the real-life grass field. Athletes were supposed to be able to run faster on the AstroTurf surface, and water puddles from inclement weather were to disappear to nonexistence.

When the "Marching 110" got that news from Mr. Richardson, we felt as though we were back at the "Top-Of-The-Heap."

Our "Bass-Drum" players, Calvin Powell and Mike Thrift were 6 feet tall each, with some bulk, and both of them could "Whale-Their-Bass-Drums". There were times when paths needed to be cleared for the band to march through the crowds of onlookers and fans. Another of the "Drum-Section's" job was to clear the path. Usually the "Snare-Drum's" would lead the way, but for this special ocassion which required a "special-path-to-be-made," the "Perecussion-Line-Up" had to be changed, and the bass drummers would lead and clear the way. If you wanted to see any bass drum player handle their instrument with skill and prowess, Mike and Calvin were the epitome. They were a tandem all by themselves, performing in conjunction with each other. They could work it. They would twirl and swing those big bass drums like they were nothing to lift, at the same time whaling all the way with their long-extended arms. Onlookers would have to disperse when they saw Calvin and Mike coming their way.

When we got to "Veterans Stadium", for that Sunday's football game, the band had to line up in the tunnel that ran underneath of the stadium. The tunnel led to the entrance onto the stadium's floor, sort of like the back stage entrance for a high school auditorium. The band lined up, not in a full band formation, but in a two-line column formation facing the uphill processional to the entrance. We gathered ourselves in preparation to enter the stadium and perform a half-time show for the Philadelphia Eagles and the Washington Redskins.

The closer we got to the narrowing of the tunnels entrance, the louder the fan noise became. The noise got so loud that the band couldn't hear itself. Because of the acoustics and the shear excitement of the fans, we couldn't hear the whistle tweets of Rusty's whistle, and the band couldn't hear the distinction in the cadence rhythm it needed to gage its stepping off timing.

The "Drum-Section" was lined up in the middle of the double-lined column. Mr. Richardson along with Rusty motioned, calling the "Drum-Section" to the front of the bands's "Double-Lined" column line-up. When we got to the front of the band and stood there at the fields' entrance, fans were waving their hands above the entrance, shouting and leaning over the entrance door from the top of the entrance and around both sides. It was pandemonium.

The drum section, in turn, made a change in its line-up and moved the bass drum players to the front of the drumline and in front of the entire band. When the bass drummers got in place, we knew that we could cut through that noise. The fans were off the hook, and there was no let-up in their fandemonium. The closer we got to the stadium's floor level field entrance, the louder the fans' frenzy became.

Rusty gave five whistle tweets which the band never heard. Along with those whistle tweets came five up and down movements with Rusty's drum major baton. Mike and Calvin and the rest of the band knew that we were stepping off. They took the band through that noise, whaling and making a path through the additional fans standing just inside on the stadium floor. They had to clear a path when they saw Calvin and Mike moving their way. When the 110 got inside of the stadium, the fan noise and hoopla became grander and more robust. The half-time show was the Marching 110s' to conquer. We always had the idea that we were one of the good marching bands around, but we never became comfortable with resting on our accomplishments. We felt that from a good performance, there was always room to take it up a notch, to higher levels of perfection.

Once inside of the stadium, the fans pushed the band, and in some sense, required of us to take it to the next stage. The half-time entrance to the field was performed with crisp double-time high-stepping movements with a drum cadence that riveted through the stadium and caught the fans fanaticism.

The seven-minute show was all it took for the Marching 110 to have that crowd in the palm our hands. The fans at Veterans Stadium really took to our style of half-time presentation. The frenzy was non-stop. Even when the band exited the field after the half-time show, the fans wanted more. They were so overwhelmed by the shear funk of our cadences and the band's marching style and energy. They fed off of our energy and we reciprocated.

Their eyes were glued to us. Even as the band re-entered the tunnel on the way out of the stadium floor, fans stood in the tunnel cheering and clapping as we marched pass. Their appreciation was so gratifying that as the "Drum-Section" led the band back through the "Stadium Tunn" some of the fans held out six packs of beer as the band passed. Mike and Calvin were in front, and never missing a beat, looked back at the rest of the "Drum -Section" and said that they weren't going to pass up the fans' offer of several "six packs of beer." It was hot, and we were dripping with sweat.

Initially, the rest of the "Drum-Section" didn't know where we were going tout those cans of beer and continue to play our drums. One of the drummers and then the rest of the "Drum-Section" grabbed a "six pack" from one of the fans and tucked it inside of the front overlay of their uniform while continuing to play all the way back through the "Stadium Tunnel."

When we exited the "Stadium Tunnel" and the "Stadium" after the "Kick-Down," already had refreshments to quench their thirst. The sound of beer cans popping as they were opened and the jubilation of triumph from band members put a cap on this, another "Marching 110" performance success.

Upon arrival at "Veterans Stadium", band members received mixed messages with regards to the "Half-Time" show being televised. Some messages said that it would be televised, and some said that it wouldn't.

No matter what the message was, the "Marching-110-Band" was already focused on producing a favorable outcome to move the band a step closer to "Legendary-Status."

It's important to note that Virginia State College and now Virginia State University was and is a co-educational college campus, and the school's band reflected the student body with male as well as female band members. These band members wore their band uniforms with a badge of pride and distinction. It was something about putting that "Trojan-Band-Uniform" on that propelled the person who wore it to "Excellence-In-Performance."

The Trojan band uniform was a medium blue, double breasted dress suit which could be worn in concert performances by not wearing the front overlay. The "Marching 110" always wore Orange & White front overlays. The pants had an orange stripe down the side and a white puffed feather pom-pom grazed the top of the hat. White cords were worn on each shoulder of the suit coat, and a white chin strap hung down to clutch your chin. Usually band members would let that chin strap hang there around the chin area which added a touch of "attitude" for showmanship. The hat also was that medium color of blue trimmed in orange with a gold emblem right in front of the hat. Band hats were pushed down on bushy Afro hair styles that peaked out underneath on the sides and around the back.

The suit coat had gold buttons with raised harps designed on the buttons with a musical emblem design at the bottom of each sleeve. The overlay had a high collar that went around the neck with an "S" on each side of the front of the collar. The overlay could be tightened or loosened with sliding claps on each side at the waist. The overlay was used for more than just to hold cans of beer.

Inside the coat's inner pocket under the overlay, snare drummers would keep an extra set of drumsticks just in case a stick was broken or fell down to the ground during the performance. Tenor drummers also kept a mallet or two in their coat's inside pocket under the overlay. Bass drum players would keep one large mallet under their overlay.

White gloves were worn by all band members, except the drum

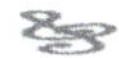

section. Black shoes were worn with white spats over them in order to help to accentuate the high stepping movements.

The"Drum-Major" wore an altogrther different uniform from that of the band. The "Drum-Major" wore an all-white or cream-white uniform with orange trimmings. Orange buttons adorned it with an orange musical emblem on the bottom of each sleeve. The "Drum-Majors' " hat was like on e of those worn by the "Buckingham Palace Guards."

Majorettes wore cream-white uniforms trimmed in orange on the short pants style. There was an orange front overlay and orange tassels on white marching boots.

All of the drums in the drum section were pearl white, crystal drums, snare, tenor, bass drums, and quads. The bass drums carried the Trojan emblem on their drum hides. The emblem was the head of a Trojan warrior with the Trojan headdress. The words "Virginia State College Marching Band" was written around the outer rim of the bass drum hide in blue and orange magic marker. The Trojan head was centered in the middle of the hide in magic marker colors of blue, orange and brown for the Trojan mans face.

One bass drum had the picture of the Trojan head in the center, and the other bass drum didn't. The bass drum with the Trojan head in the center of the hide, the head could only be seen by its outer etchings. The pounding of the bass drum mallets had erased the majority of the magic marker drawing of the Trojan head. Mike and Calvin so thrived on skillfully pounding their respective bass drum.

Calvin and Mike didn't compete against one another. They played off of each other, complimenting the other's gift and genuine zeal for perfection and downright having a good time playing their"Bass-Drums." I can't mention Calvin without mentioning Mike in the same breath or Mike without mentioning Calvin. They were a formidable pair that epitomized and demonstrated to those of us in the "Drum-Section" what it meant to be "Team" players along with the tenacity that was needed to be "Trojan" drummers.

The second performance for the "Marching 110," in the Fall of

1972, was in support of our "Trojan" Football team in the "Ujima Football Classic." None of the band members had ever heard of the "Ujima Classic," but we were all excited to be invited to perform in support of our football team where the opponent was "Delaware State College" out of Dover, Deleware, another HBCU. It was an African American football clash of titans in Hartford, CT. All we knew was, since we didn't get invited back to "Yankee Stadium", "Hartford" was in the direction of New York City, and we were alright with that.

The "Marching 110" traveled to the "Ujima Classic," not knowing what to expect in terms of fan attendance and the size of the stadium where the game would be played. We later learned that there was a high Virginia State alumni following in the Hartford area, and they really showed out for the game. There was a popular set of twins who were from Hartford and were Virginia State cheerleaders who had just graduated the previous year that helped to welcome the band to the Hartford area and helped the bus drivers maneuver around by sitting in the front of the bus and standing in the "step-aboard" area pointing out directions.

When we got to the stadium, we noticed that Delaware State's band wasn't there. When the band saw that and especially the "Drum-Section," the talk was that we were going to take our performance to "Beyond-Kick-Down-VSC"and take it to the fans. We were going to have to cover Delaware State's band, who hadn't made the trip, and definitely for the Trojan fan base, as we knew that our football team would take care of business.

As expected, our football team took care of business by defeating Delaware State, and the band performed masterfully at half-time. The drum section brought the band off of the field with funk beats all the way back into the stands.

Word went down through the "Drum-Section" was to play every cadence with a funkier beat and rhythm than usual. As the"Drum-Section" started to get into the stands, we hit it off early wth the "African Munbo" cadence and kept the groove going even when the cadence changed. The African Mumbo cadence was usually saved for the "Drumline's" Kick-Down-VSC" showdown, but we changed the cadence order moving it up to when the band was getting to their seats just after half-time, and all of the sections got into it and set off the funk right there in the stands, the "Drum-Section" realized that this was an "African American Classic" setting and that we didn't have a music building or a place to go after the game to bring on "Beyond -Kick-Down-VSC," and there was no rival band to compete against. We just had to bring it on ourselves. It was just the right touch. The fans went wild and ate it up. As the game went on through the third and fourth quarters, the fans wouldn't let us stop the rhythms. That was okay with the "Drum-Setion". and we loved every bit of the pandemonium and continued to jam on.

The bleachers weren't as high as some high school stands that you might see, which lent itself to easy access to the band by the fans. Once the football game was over, the band remained in the stands, and fans just stood there looking at us in appreciation. To our surprise, droves of boys managed to make it up to the top of the stands where the drum section was seated. They got to the "Drum-Section" an dbrought out paper and pens with event posters and programs for the drum section to sign our personal autographs. They began passing the paper and pens down the side of the bleachers to boys standing on the ground. They didn't impede our playing, but their faces and expressions were lit up with joy as the rhythms continued while we signed autographs. The drum section felt that those boys showed us one of the highest forms of respect and appreciation that we had received for any performance. We played even that much harder.

That exchange of the boys initiating the autograph signing of the "Marching 110 Drum-Section" moved the "Drum-Section" from "Beyond-Kick-Down-VSC" to "Celebity Status" capping our progression in "Percussion-Lore" bragging rights as one of the best , of any college "Drum-Section" in the land. The "Drum-Section" loved it because they were allowed to come right up to us and weren't turned away by Rusty or Mr. Richardson. I don't think they could have stopped their excitement or exuberance if they tried.

The Ujima Football Classic in Hartford, CT, is forever etched in the hearts and spirits of the Men and Women ot the "1972- Marching-110-Band and "Drum-Section." It's a testimony of the "Marching-

110-Drum-Section's" exceptional performance of "foot-stomping", "spin-tingling", "hair-raising",and "electrifying display of rhythm and routine as to the way audiences received them.

The "Marching 110" not only performed at "professional football" "Half-Time" shows and "high-profile away engagements," but the band was a fixture in the Petersburg, Virginia area holiday parades. Also, the "Marching 110" was involved in inspiring and enhancing the high school marching band experience by hosting 'High School Band" days on "the Hill" at Rogers Stadium. Local high school bands were invited to the high school band dayextraaganza to observe the"Marching 110's" performance and to participate by offering their own half-time show. For these events, "Mattoaca High Schools" marching band with their Red and White uniforms and "Petersburg High School" with their Maroon and White band uniforms were regularly welcomed guests of the "Marching 110."

Mr. Richardson's son, young Claiborne Richardson, was the member of the "Drum-Section" who I believed really kept the"Drum-Section" grounded by his prescence. He was about 11 or 12 years old and was all but pleased as punch to be hanging out with the "Marching 110" as a member of it's "Drum-Section." As part of the drum section, Claiborne, in some sense, helped us to remain down to earth and not dwell on being this college level "Drum-Secton" in this great marching machine known as the "Maching 110." Though his daddy, Mr. Richardson, put him up to it, he was more than glad to play his cymbals while enjoying the ride of always performing "On-The-Brink."

Claiborne wore an all-white outfit of pants, sweat shirt, tennis shoes with a cotton skull cap. We never heard a word of discord from him. Neither did Mr. Richardson have to say a word of reprimand as discipline to him. I believe I heard Mr. Richardson speak of Claiborne in conversation before the assembly of the band in the band room only on one occasion. He just came and played his cymbals, which were a smaller version of the larger held cymbals; then he went home.

The unique thing about the "Marching 110" "Drum-Section" that set it apart was that all of its cadences were meant to be played while the section was in some sort of movement. Once the drum section

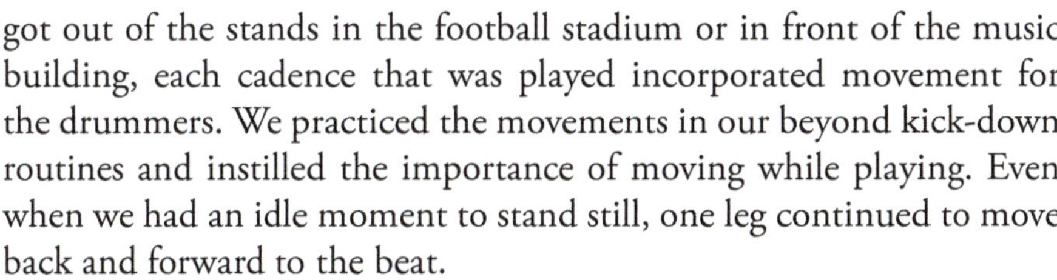

got out of the stands in the football stadium or in front of the music building, each cadence that was played incorporated movement for the drummers. We practiced the movements in our beyond kick-down routines and instilled the importance of moving while playing. Even when we had an idle moment to stand still, one leg continued to move back and forward to the beat.

African Drum Research:

In "Roots," Kunta Kinte was taken into slavery, across the middle passage, when he was out looking for wood to make a drum. The African drum has taken on a new connotation with radio talk shows sounding the alarm and driving the beat for African American community issues and concerns.

Nobody does the "Percussion Drum Section Experience" of "Drumline" like the sons and daughters of the "African Diaspora." It is exceptional in its conception and serves as an oddity in cultural expression. Playing a percussion instrument in an HBCU gives the percussionist a feeling of being in the center of African culture.

Drummers, by nature, whether they are aware of it or not, tend to want to be heard. They play their percussion instrument to be heard. Therefore, beginners will strike their drum heads and beat on their drum hides too hard. The focus is to develop their skill level by concentrating on striking the drum sticks head in the center of the drum hide. Snare drummers will hit around the outer sides of the drum head which produces a distorted sound and, in some instances, break or rip the drum head.

The secret to the success of skillful drumming is to cultivate the proper usage of your wrist action. Don't bang on the drum head but skillfully aim for the center of the drum hide for a fuller sound.

These pages are written as a documentary to the origins of the drumline as it derived exclusively within the African American HBCU genre.

Prior to 1971, there was no competition between opposing school's percussion sections. As "Captain" of the "Drum-Section" of the

"Virginia State College Marching 110 Band" of Petresburg, Virginia in 1973 and member of the "Drum-Section" from 1971-1973, the "Drum-Section" claims the "Bragging Rights" for laying down the ground work of starting and establishing what is now known as "The Drumline"!!!

For the "Drum-Section" of the "Virginia State College Marching 110 Band" each performance built our skill and confidence for pushing the envelope on the college level. Each freshman drummer of 1971 brought his sense of accomplishment with him from their respective "high school band experience" which "mushroomed" when we go to "the Hill." The only place for this "Drum-Section" to go after going "On-The-Brink" was to go "Beyond-Kick-Down-VSC" to "Legends" in "African American Percussion" "Lore-of-Innovation." This places the"Virginia State College Marching 110 Band" and "Drum-Section" from 1971-1973 as one of the"Top-Tier" "Nationally Ranked" powerhouse collegiate bands in the country. I would say that the 1971-1973 VSC?VSU "Drum-Section/Drumline" took the"Marching 110 along with the "Jammin' City Of Troy" to the "Land of Funk."

AUTHOR'S EPILOGUE NOTE: Marching Bands and Drum-Sections in particularly, need not worry about attracting an audience. When the band, no matter of the size, follows the disciplined musicianship and the "Drum-Section holds fast to the skills of "Rudimentary Instrumentation" on their percussion instruments, the audience will hear and take note of your sense of constructive bandmanship, and then the appropriate reputation will be your legacy.

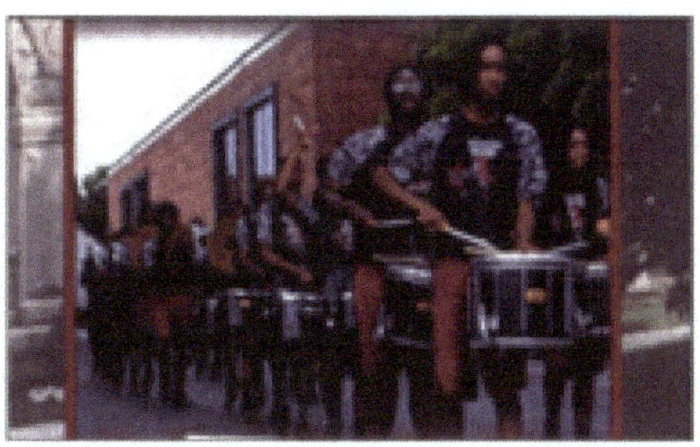

Virginia Union University, "Panthers", Richmond, Va

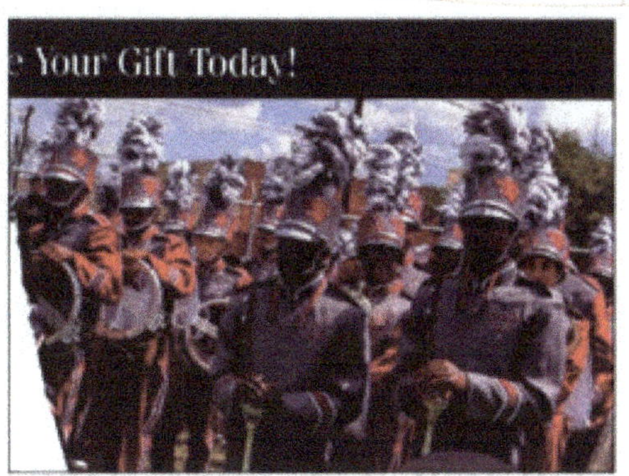

Virgina Union University, "Panthers", Richmond, Va

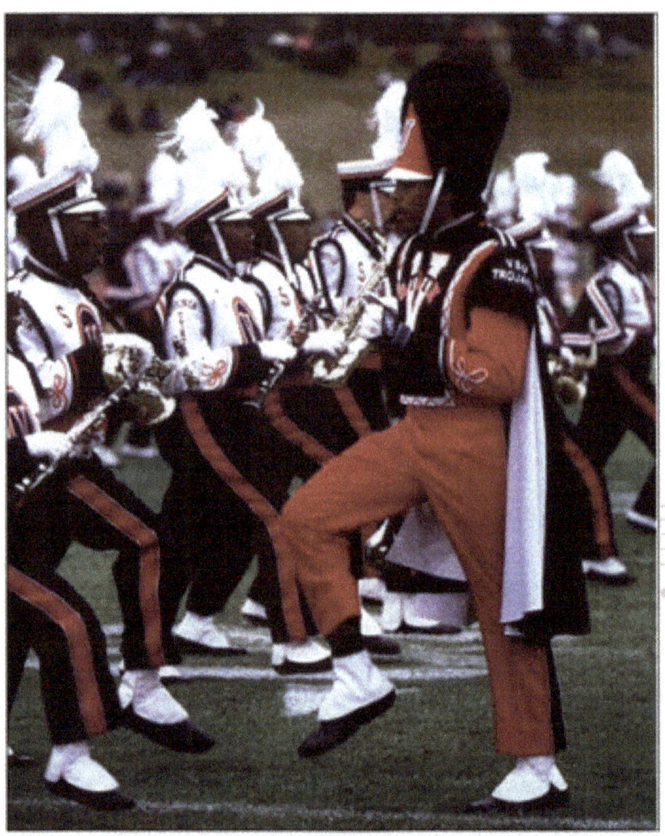

Virginia State University, "Trojans", Petersurg, Va

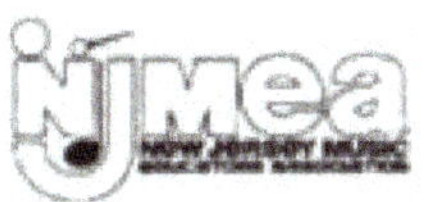

Snare Drum Rudiments

All rudiments must be memorized

Category A.

Multiple Bounce, Closed, Buzzed, Long Roll

Play for 15 seconds

pp ——— *ff* ——— *pp*

Category B.

SINGLE STROKE ROLL

(This example does not show the actual number of strokes to be played)

Play for 15 seconds

pp ——— *ff* ——— *pp*

SINGLE STROKE FOUR

8x's Cresc.
8x's Dim

L R L R   L R L R
R L R L   R L R L

FIVE STROKE ROLL

8x's Cresc.
8x's Dim

SEVEN STROKE ROLL

8x's Cresc.
8x's Dim

NINE STROKE ROLL

8x's Cresc.
8x's Dim

Category B Rudiments are to be played as quickly as possible

Category C.

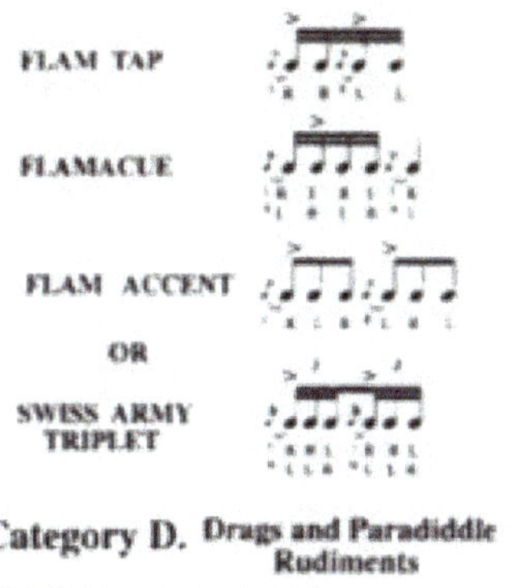

Flam Rudiments

FLAM

FLAM TAP

FLAMACUE

FLAM ACCENT

OR

SWISS ARMY TRIPLET

Category D. Drags and Paradiddle Rudiments

All Drags are to be played closed

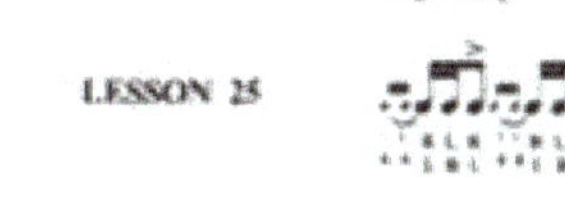

DRAG

LESSON 25

SINGLE RATAMACUE

SINGLE PARADIDDLE

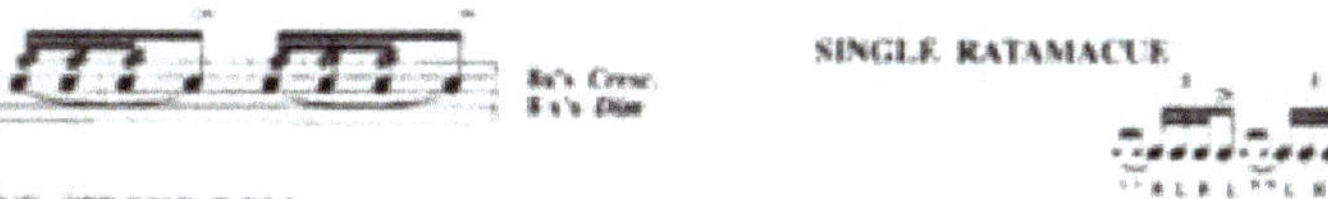

Category C & D Rudiments are to played slowly (P)
accellerando to fast, > to pp, < to ff then ritard

© 2000 N.J.M.E.A.

81

PAS International Drum Rudiments

P

PERCUSSIVE ARTS SOCIETY INTERNATIONAL DRUM RUDIMENTS

All rudiments should be practiced: open (slow) to close (fast) to open (slow) and/or at an even moderate march tempo.

I. ROLL RUDIMENTS

NEXT PAGE

A. Single Stroke Roll Rudiments

1. SINGLE STROKE ROLL *

10. NINE STROKE ROLL *

2. SINGLE STROKE FOUR

11. TEN STROKE ROLL *

3. SINGLE STROKE SEVEN

12. ELEVEN STROKE ROLL *

B. MULTIPLE BOUNCE ROLL RUDIMENTS

13. THIRTEEN STROKE ROLL *

4. MULTIPLE BOUNCE ROLL

14. FIFTEEN STROKE ROLL

5. TRIPLE STROKE ROLL

15. SEVENTEEN STROKE ROLL

C. DOUBLE STROKE OPEN ROLL RUDIMENTS

II. DIDDLE RUDIMENTS

6. DOUBLE STROKE OPEN ROLL *

16. SINGLE PARADIDDLE *

7. FIVE STROKE ROLL

17. DOUBLE PARADIDDLE *

8. SIX STROKE ROLL

18. TRIPLE PARADIDDLE

9. SEVEN STROKE ROLL *

19. SINGLE PARADIDDLE-DIDDLE

* These rudiments are also included in the original Standard 26 American Drum Rudiments

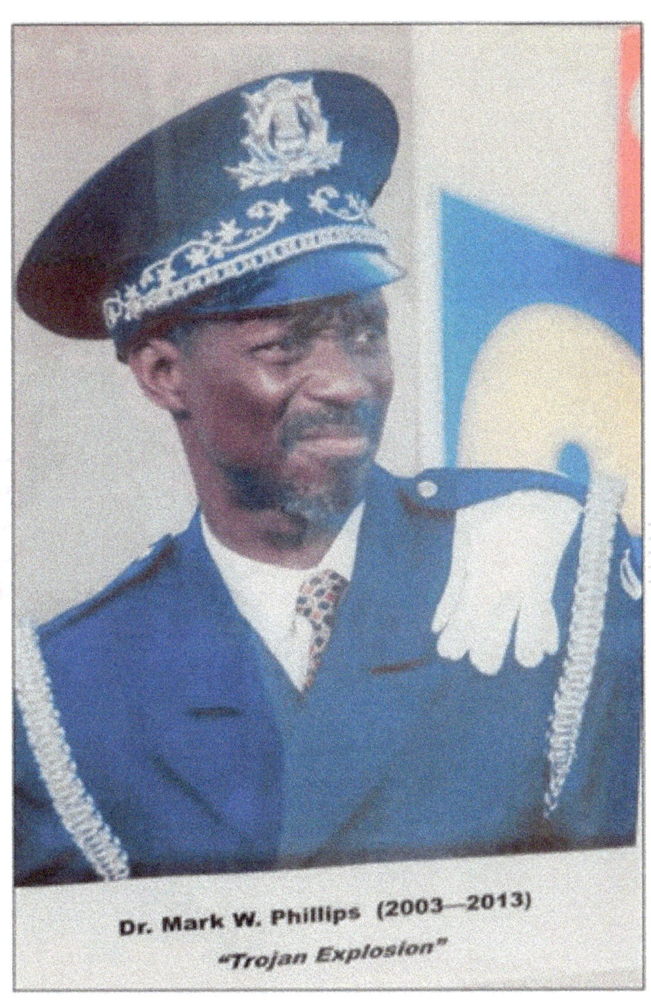

Dr. Mark W. Phillips (2003—2013)

"Trojan Explosion"

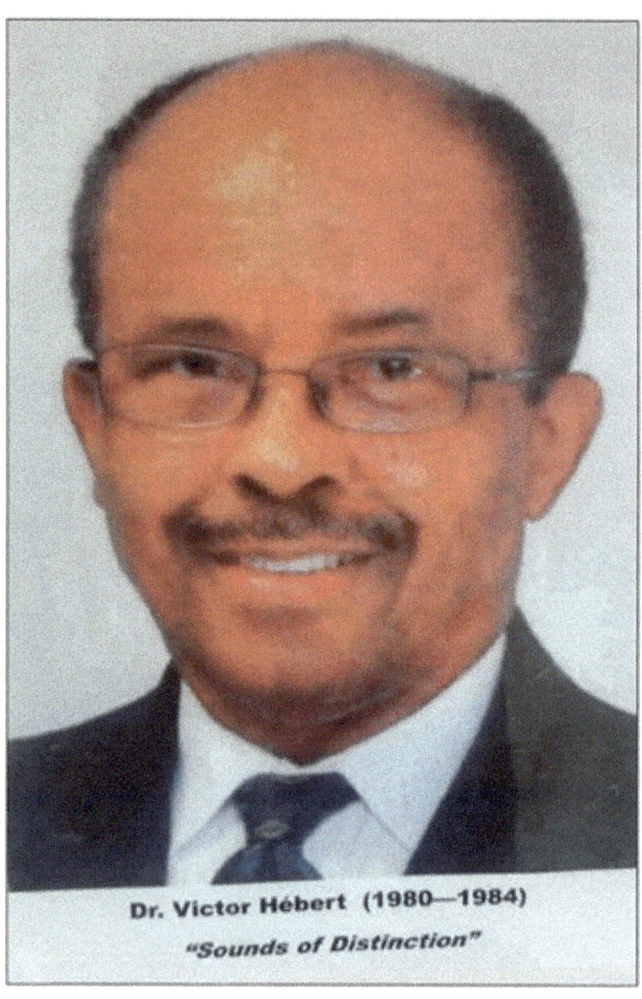

Dr. Victor Hébert (1980—1984)

"Sounds of Distinction"

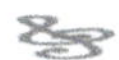

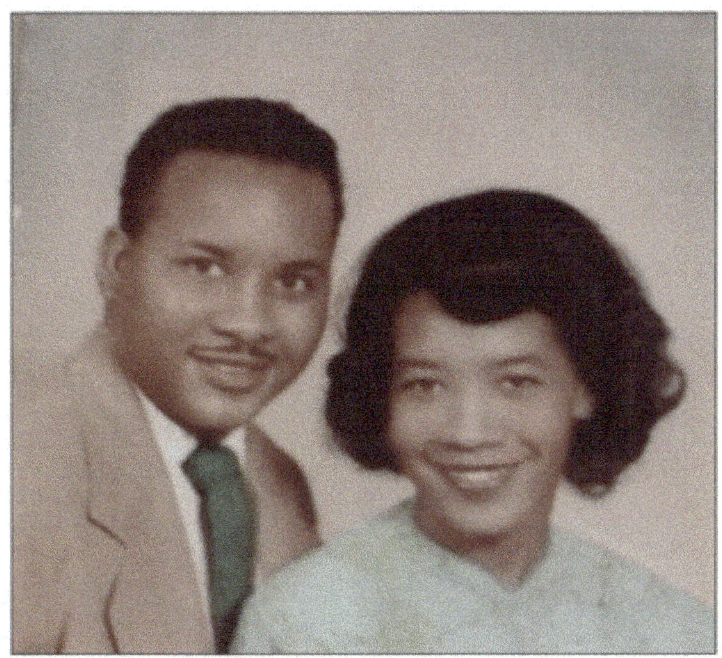

"My parents, Mr. & Mrs. Milton L. Cox, Sr.; Hampton Roads, Virginia, "I'd like to think that they are aware of this project and are cheering me on!" Circa 1950

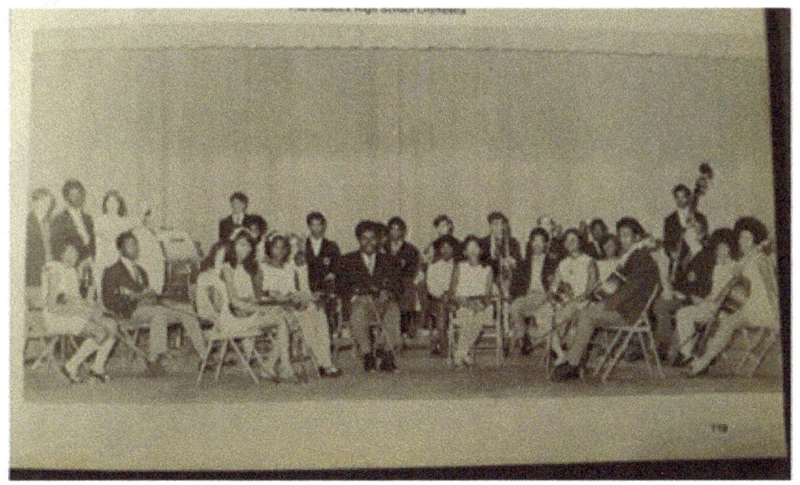

Cradock High School Orchestra, Portsmouth, Virginia, 1971.

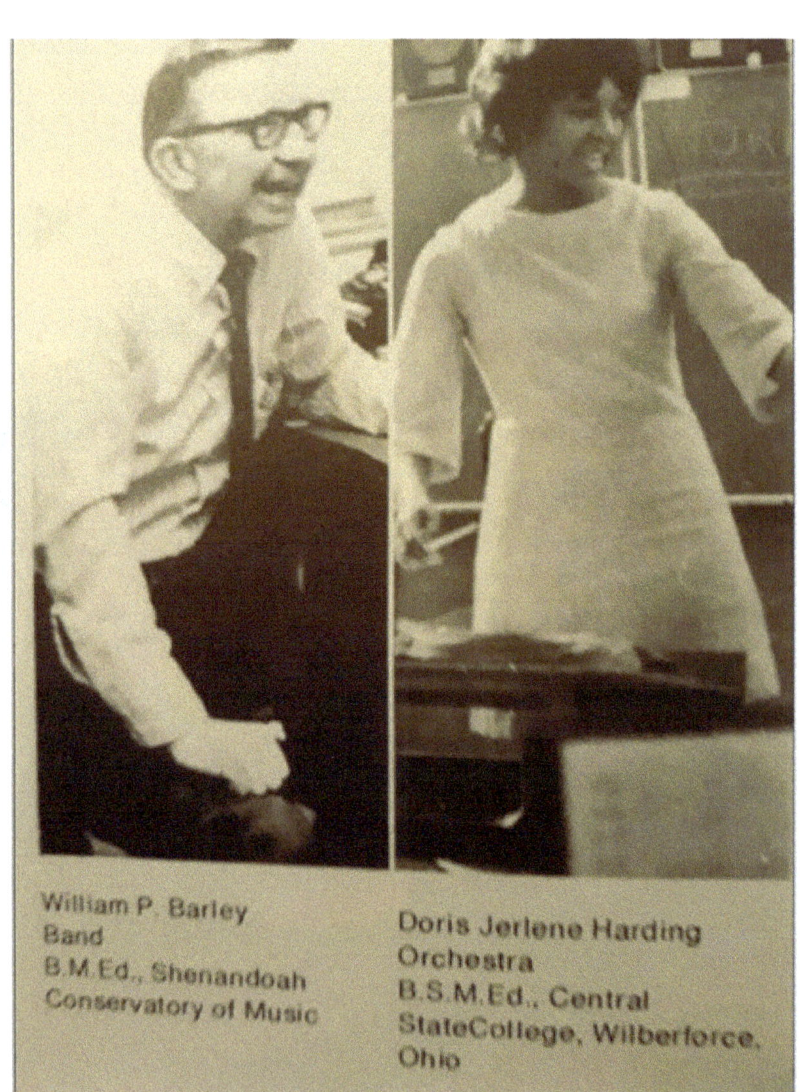

Mr. Barley & Mrs. Harding, 1971.

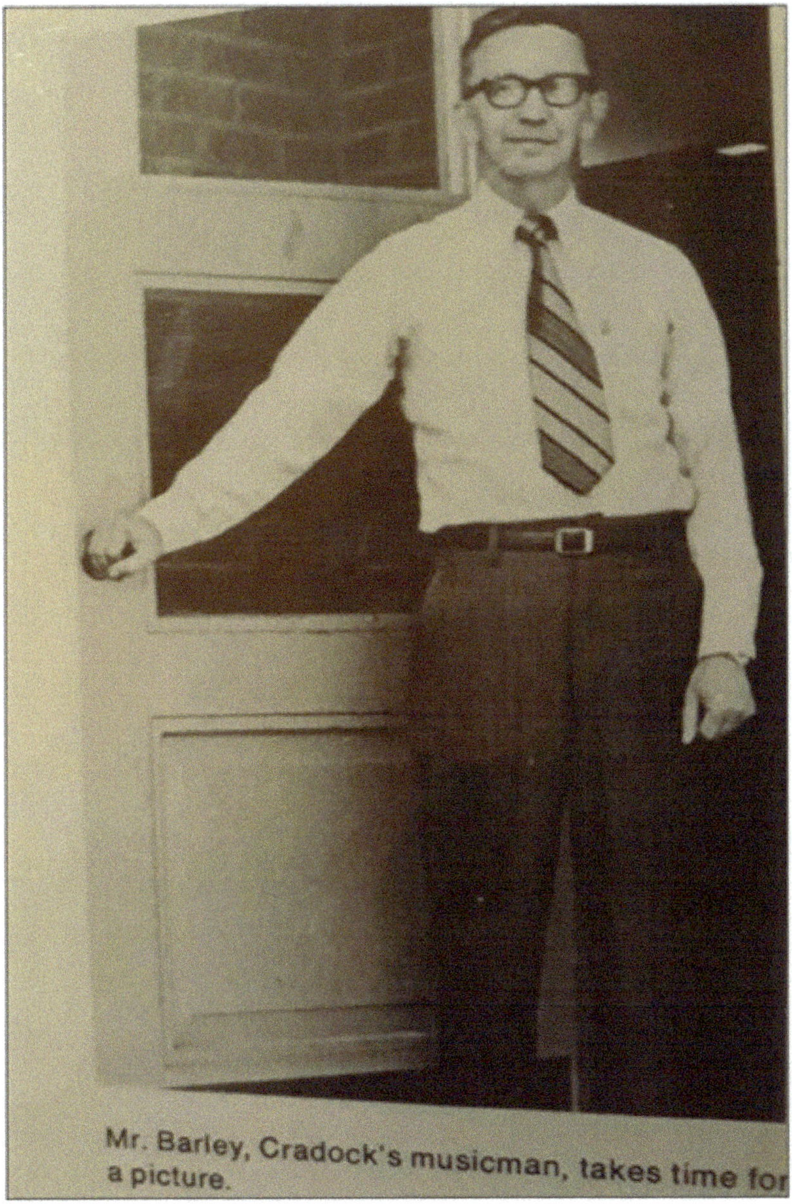

Mr. Barley, Cradock's musicman, takes time for a picture.

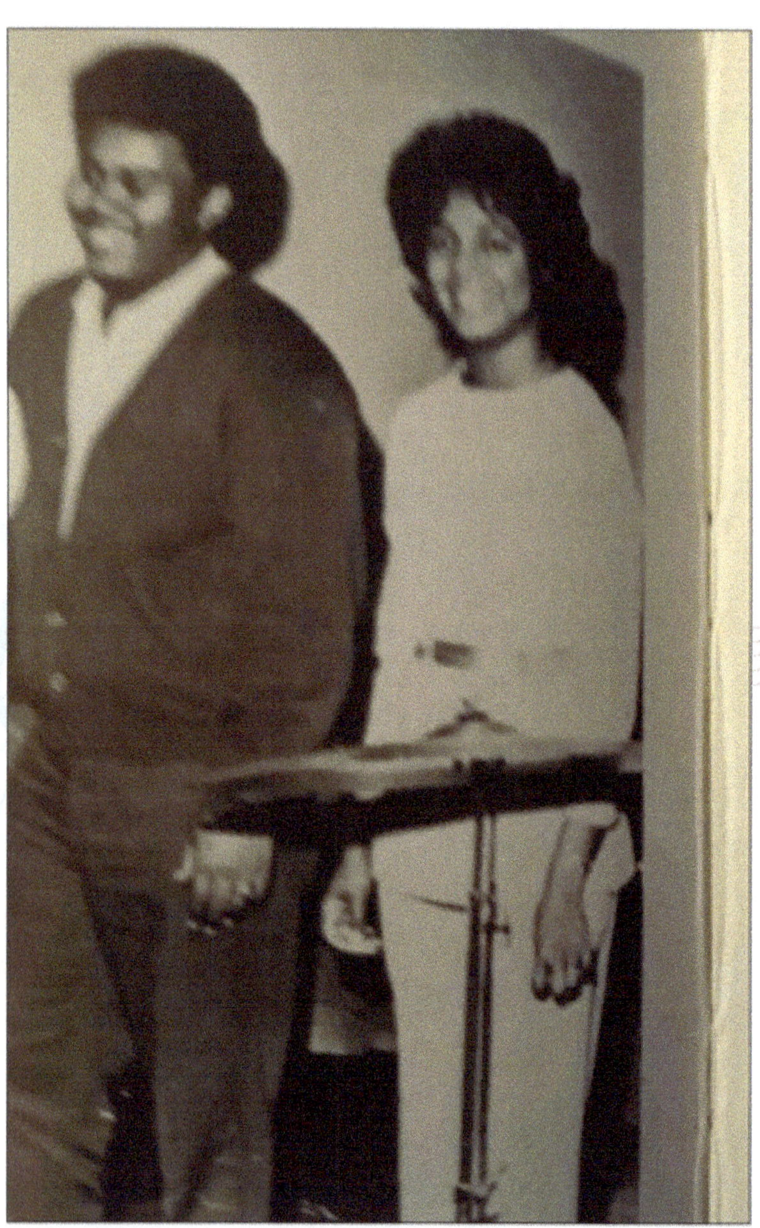

Mrs. Jerlene Harding, Cradock High School, Portsmouth, Virginia, Orchestra Director, "Simply The Best!", 1971.

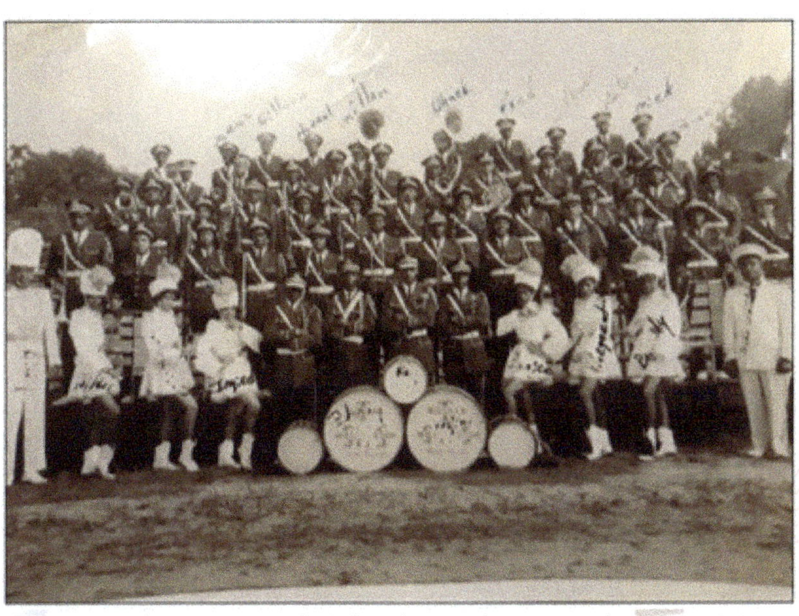

Booker T. Washington High School Marching Band, Rocky Mount, North Carolina, Circa 1965

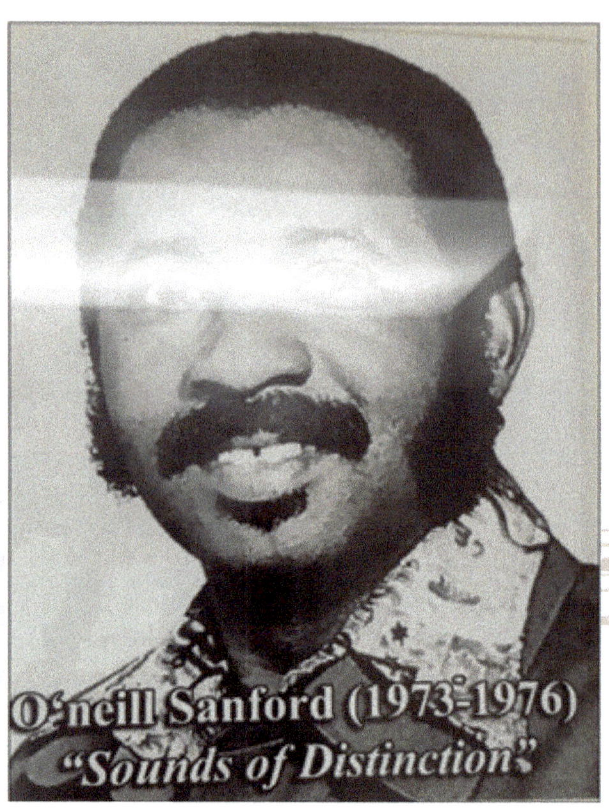
O'neill Sanford (1973-1976)
"Sounds of Distinction"

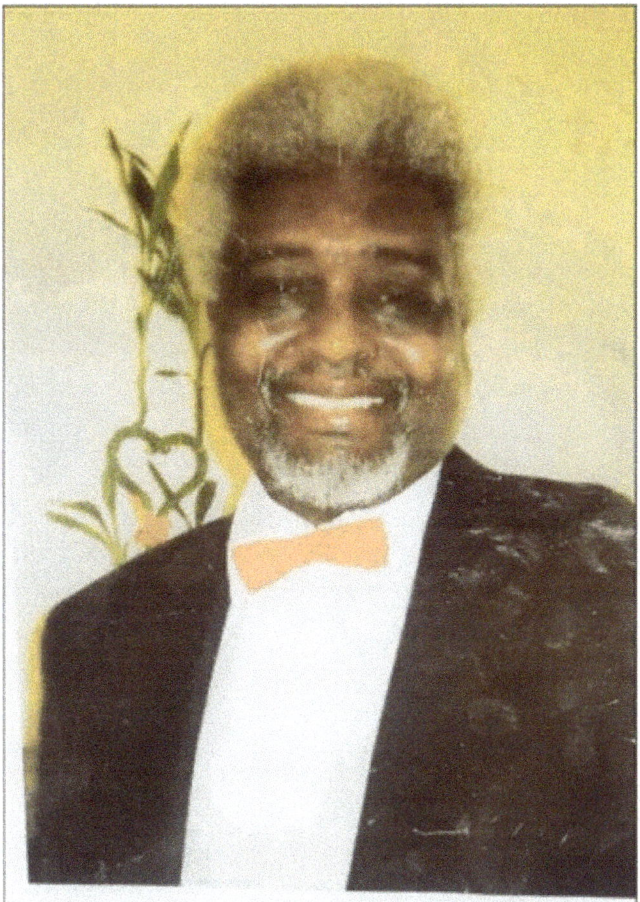

Moses Hall (1977—1980)
"Sounds of Distinction"

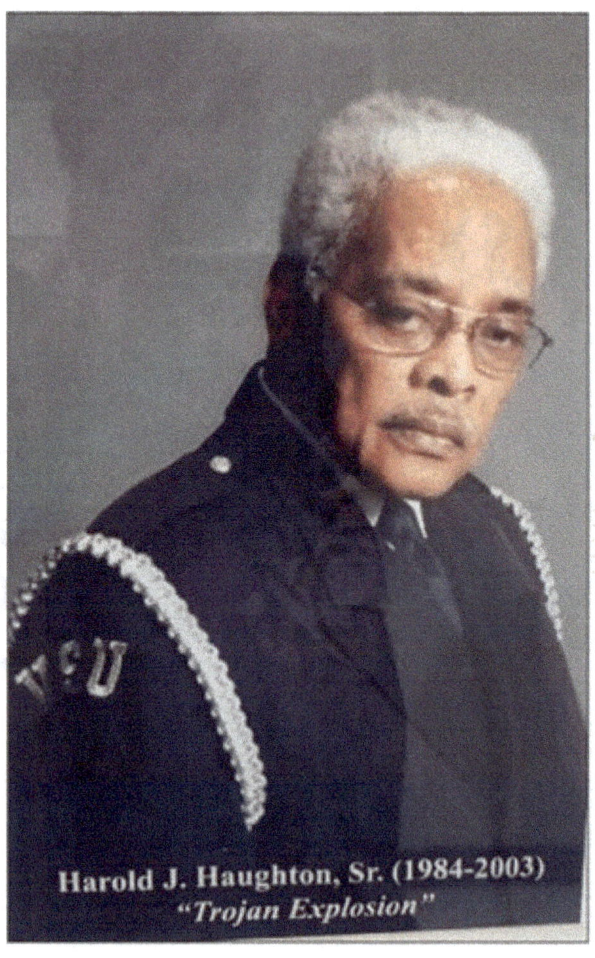

Harold J. Haughton, Sr. (1984–2003)
"Trojan Explosion"

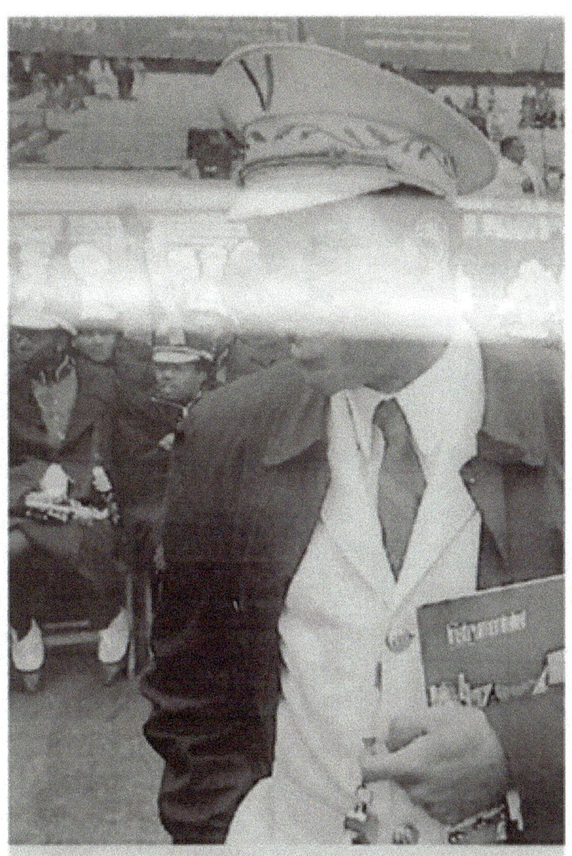

Dr. Claiborne T. Richardson

Drill Master & Assistant Conductor

"Marching 110"

1954 - 1973

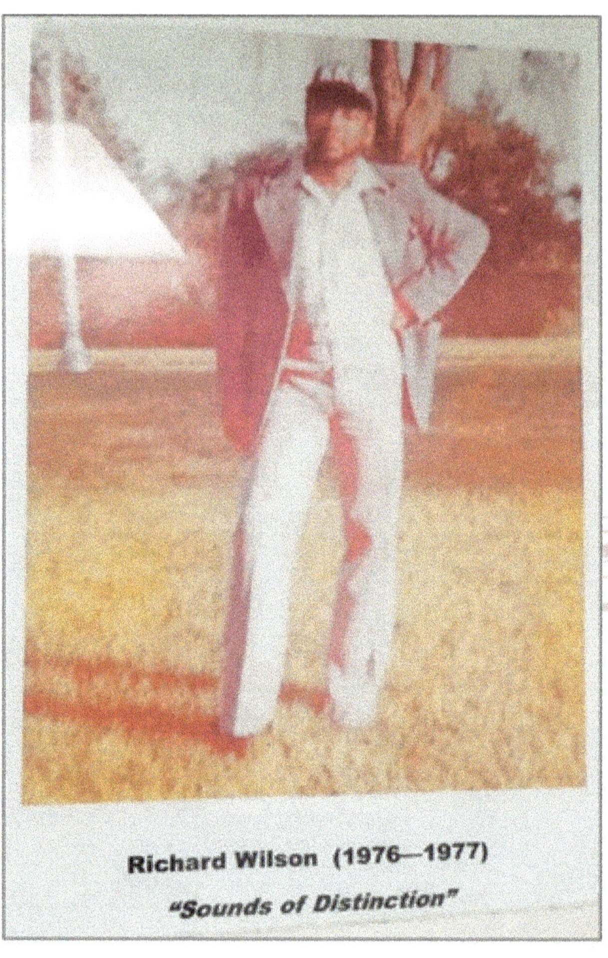

Richard Wilson (1976—1977)

"Sounds of Distinction"

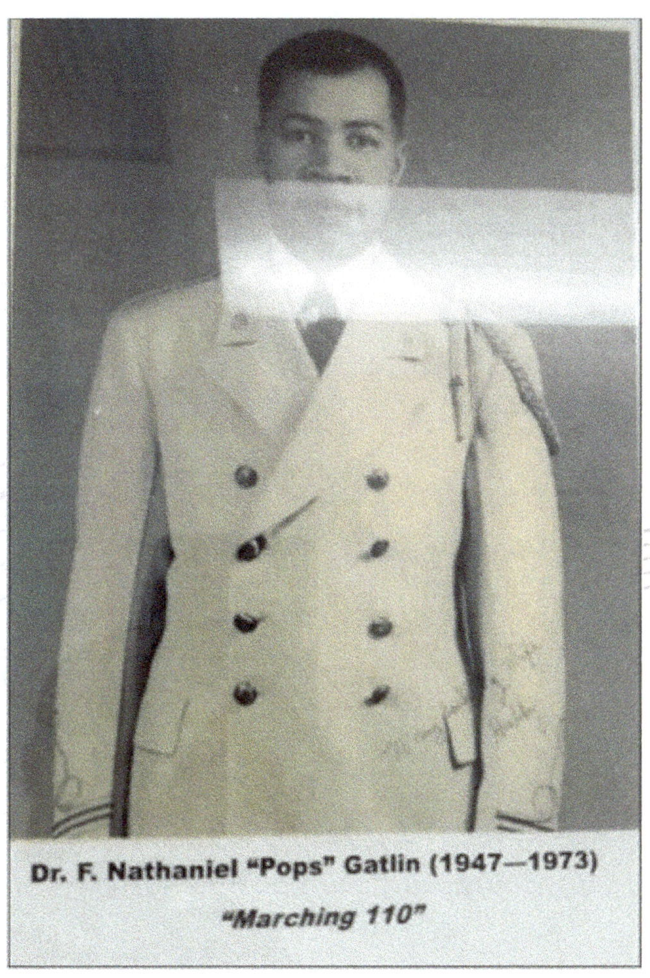

Dr. F. Nathaniel "Pops" Gatlin (1947—1973)

"Marching 110"

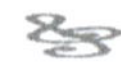

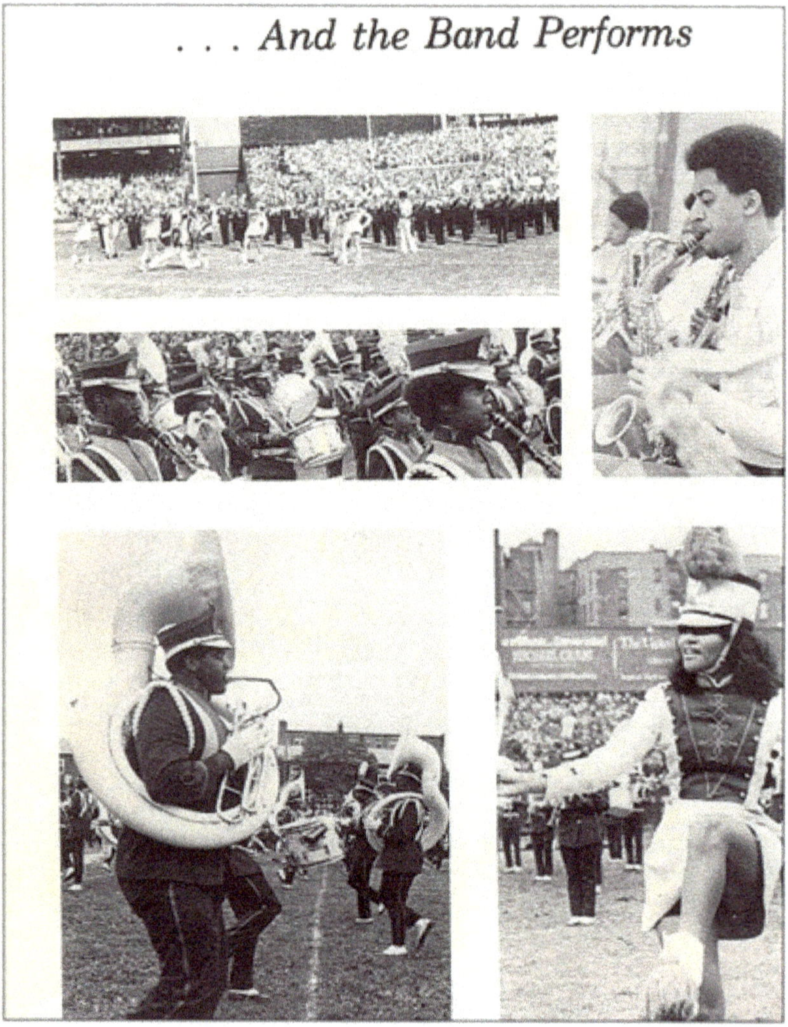

Virginia State College Marching 110, Half-Time Show, Baltimore Colts vs New York Giants, Yankee Stadium, Bronx, New York, September, 1971.

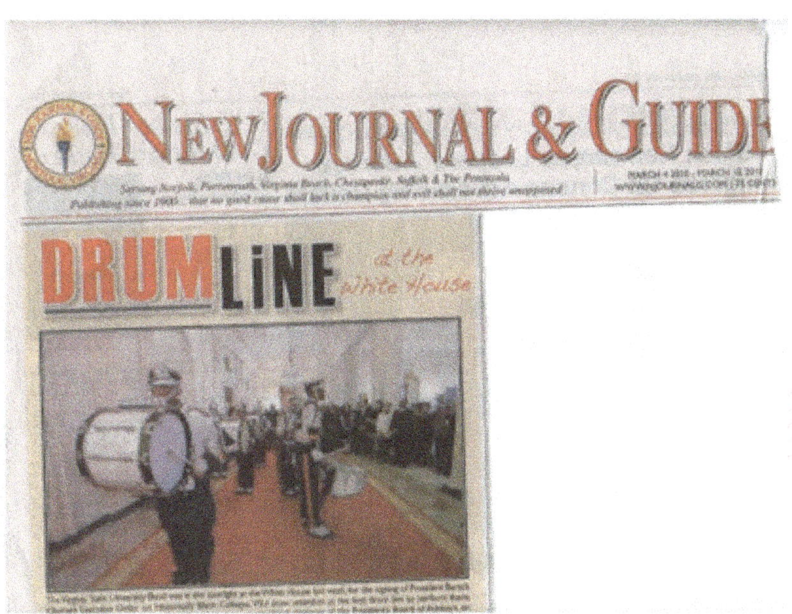

Virginia State University Drum-Line performs at the White House, 2010

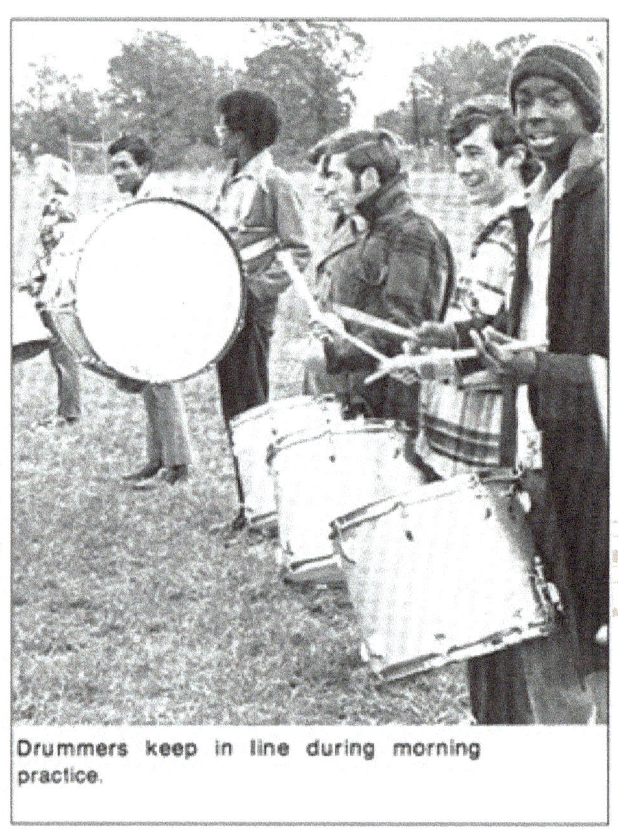

Woodrow Wilson High School, Portsmouth, Virginia, Drummers Practicing, 1972.

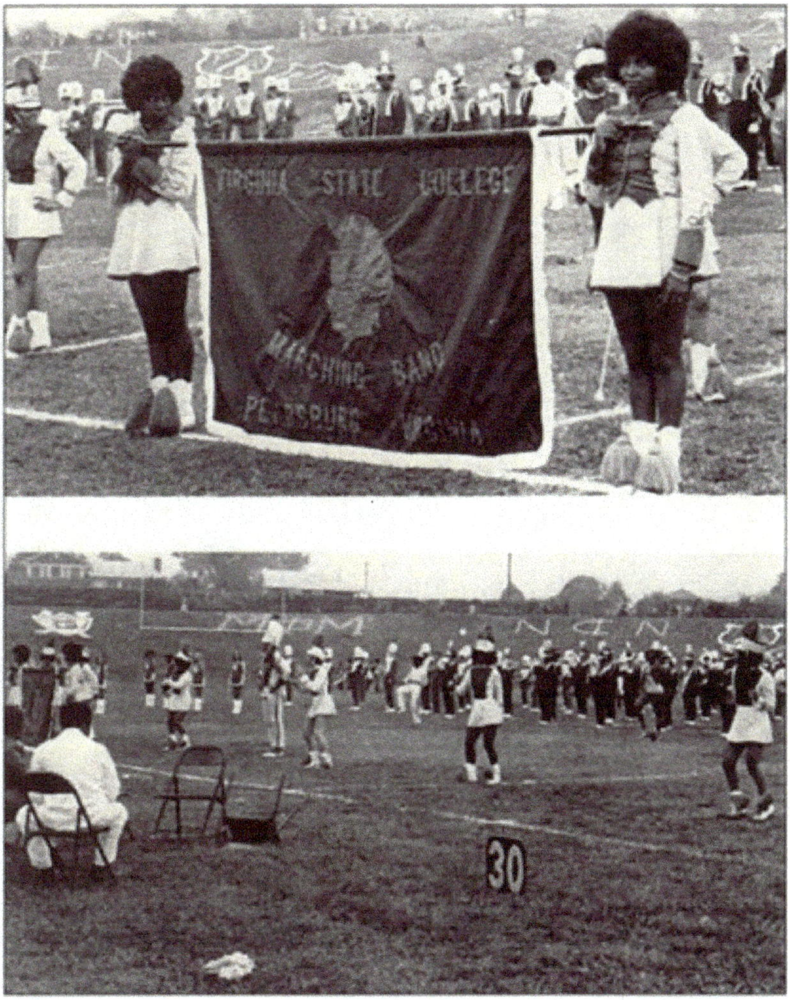

Virginia State College Marching 110, Homecoming Half-Time, Petersburg, Virginia, Circa 1971, Rogers Stadium. "Check out the Afro hair styles!"

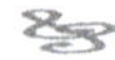

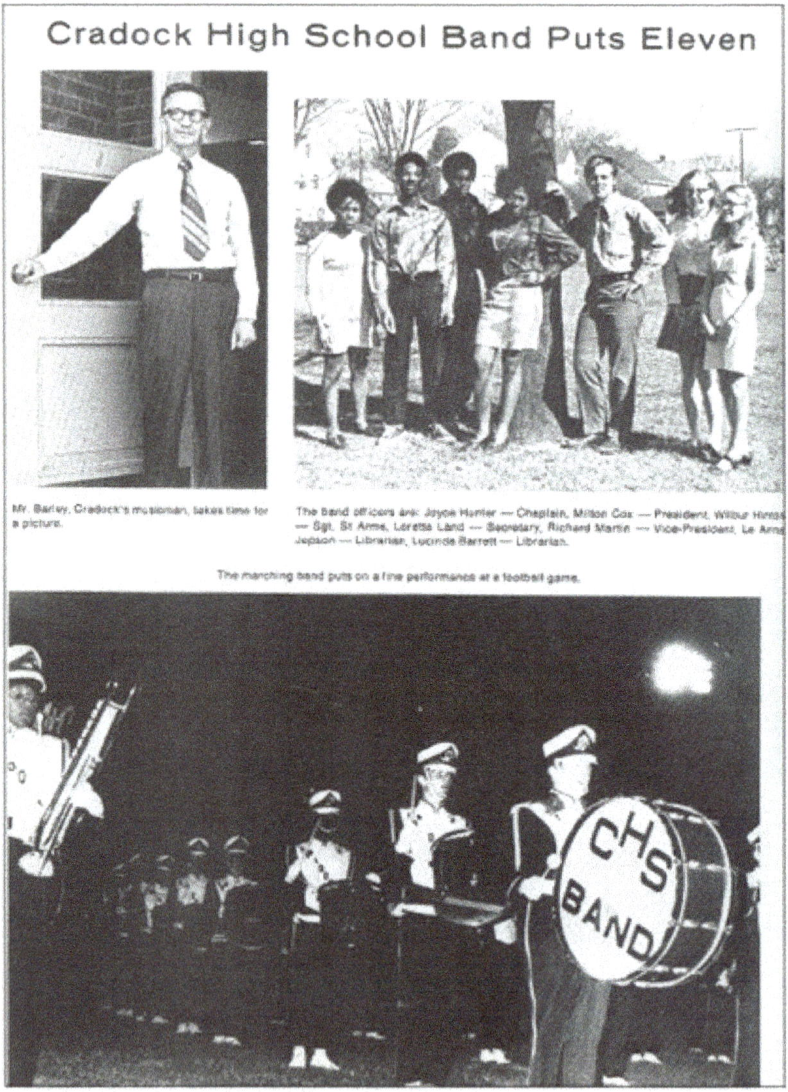

Cradock High School Marching Admirals Band, collage, Portsmouth, Virginia, 1971

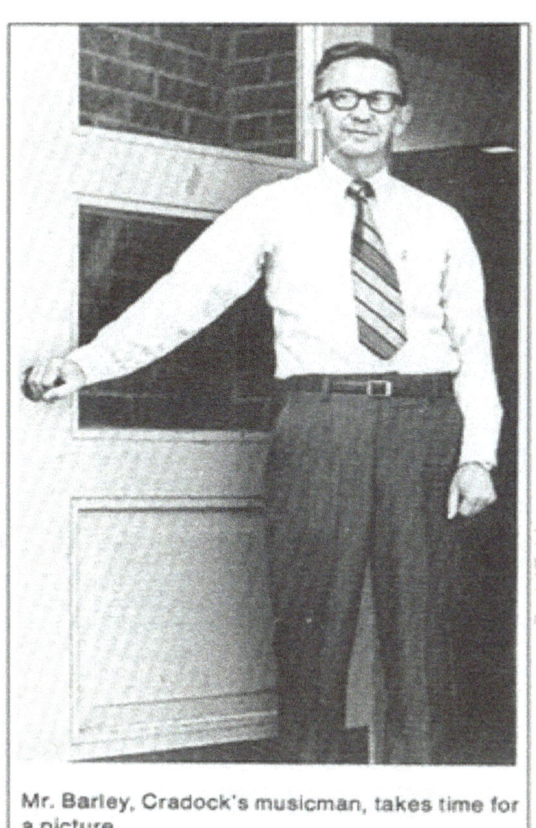

Mr. William P. Barley, Band Directory, Cradock High School, Portsmouth, Virginia, 1971. "Standing in the band room doorway!"

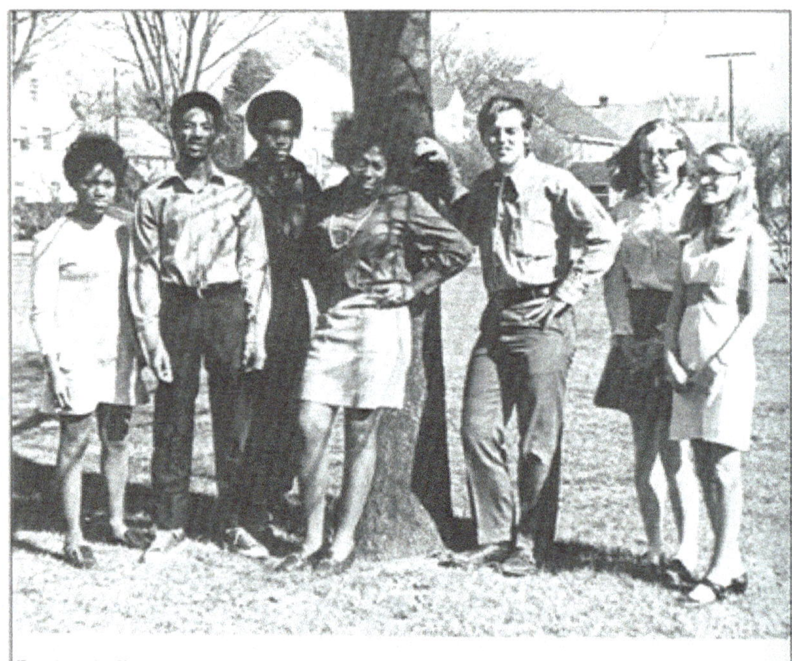

Cradock High School, Portsmouth, Virginia, "Band Officers under the tree!", 1971.

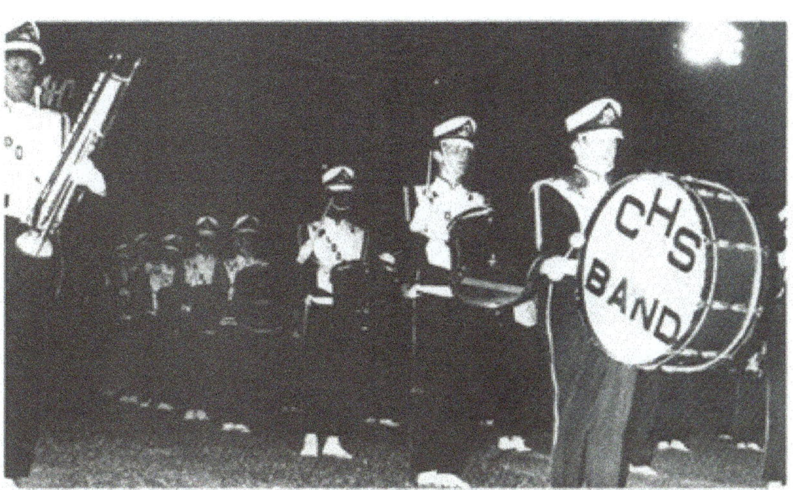

Cradock High School, Portsmouth, Virginia, Admirals Stadium, Night-Time Half-Time Show, 1971. "Yours truly, 2nd snare drummer after the bass drum!"

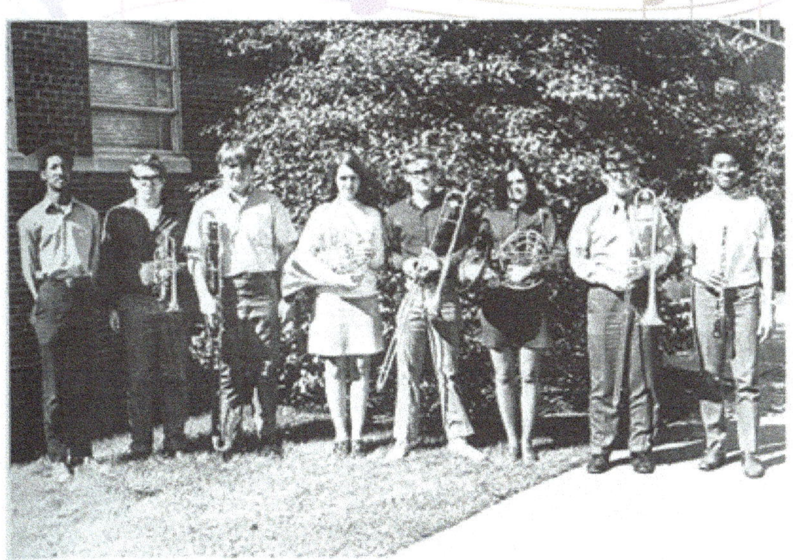

Cradock High School, Portsmouth, Virginia, Workshop Band members, " Outside of the band room!", 1971

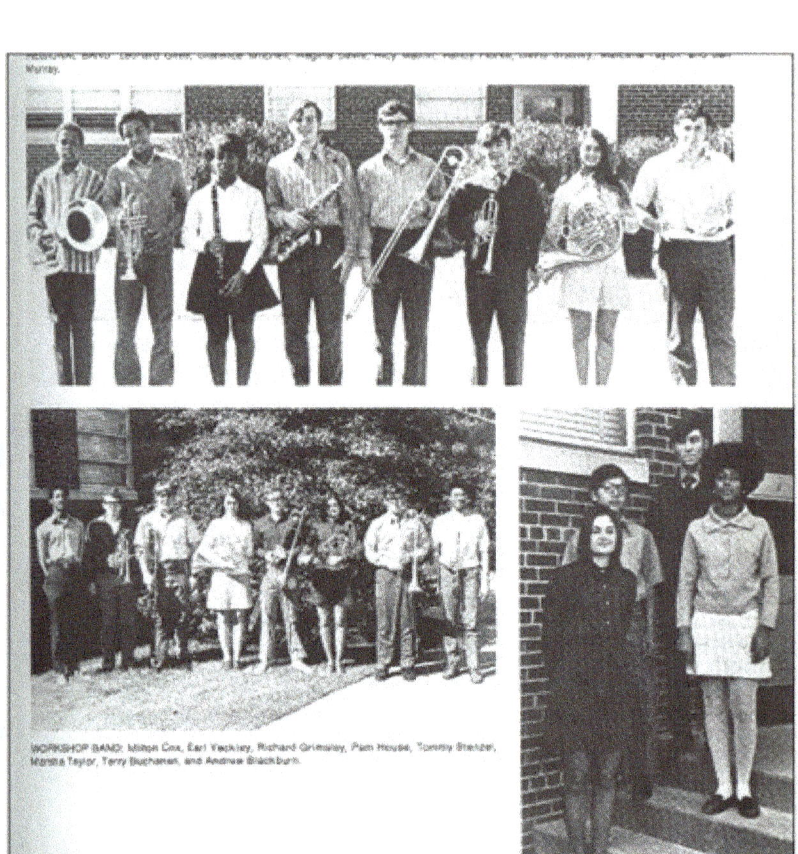

Cradock High School, Portsmouth, Virginia, Regional Band members, Workshop Band members and Band Staff, collage, " Outside of the band room!", 1971.

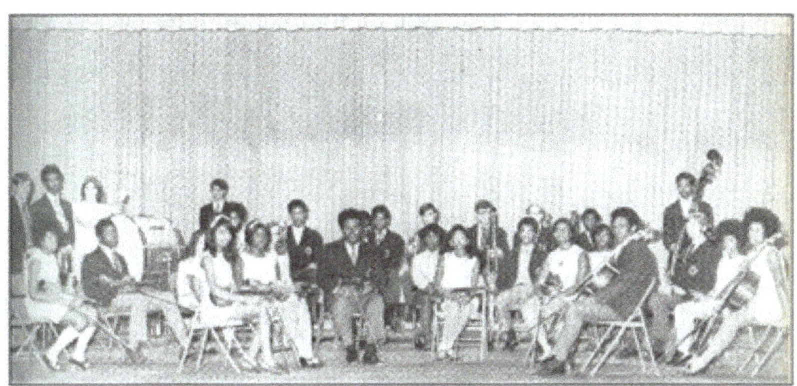

Cradock High School, Portsmouth, Virginia, Cradock High School Orchestra, "Yours truly, 1st snare drummer to the left of the bass drum!", 1971.

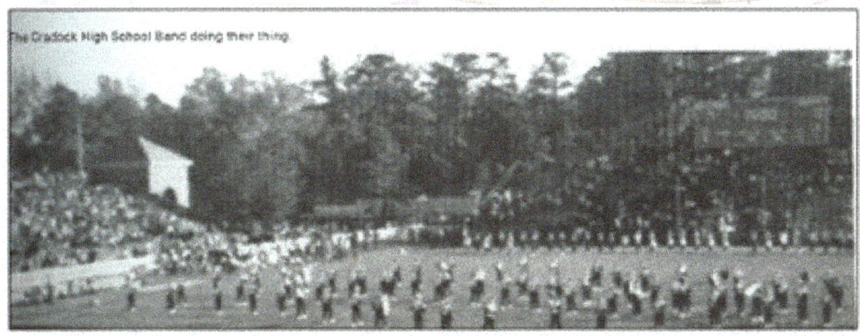

Cradock High School Marching Band, Portsmouth, Virginia, "Performs at the Virginia State Championship at The Collage of William & Mary, Williamsburg, Virginia, Moving Diamond formation!", 1971.

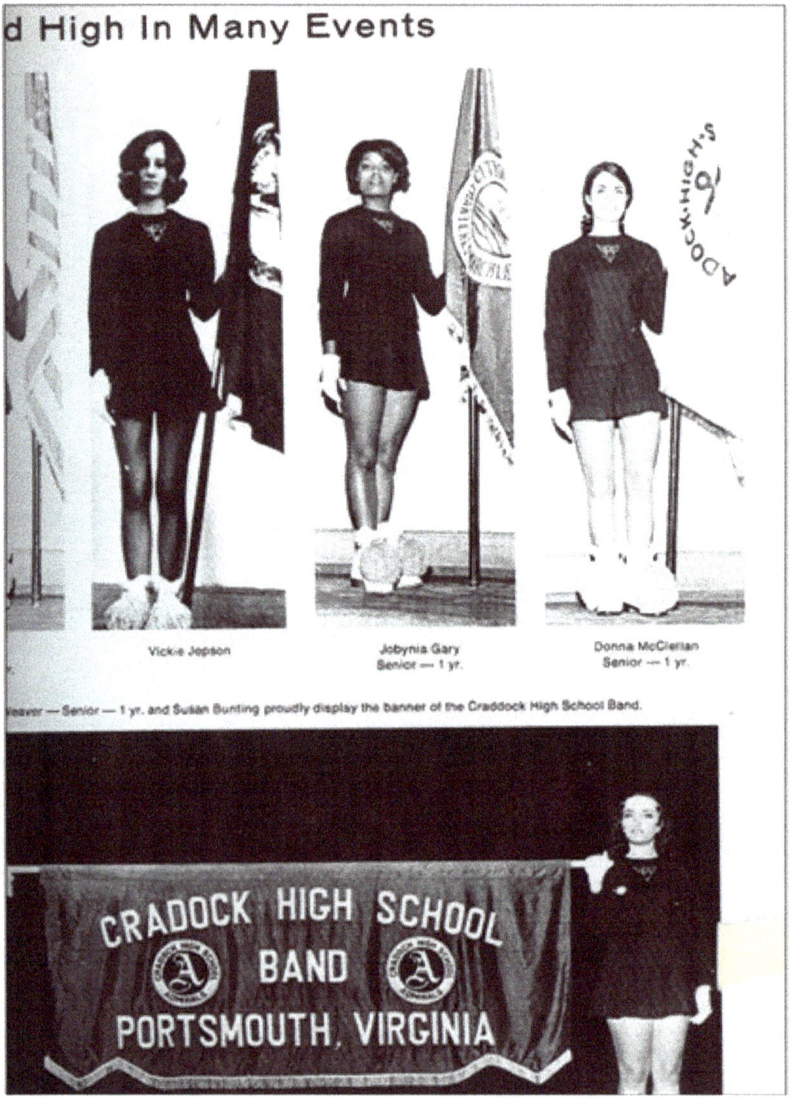

Cradock High School Marching Band, Portsmouth, Virginia, "Flag bearers and school banner, collage!", 1971.

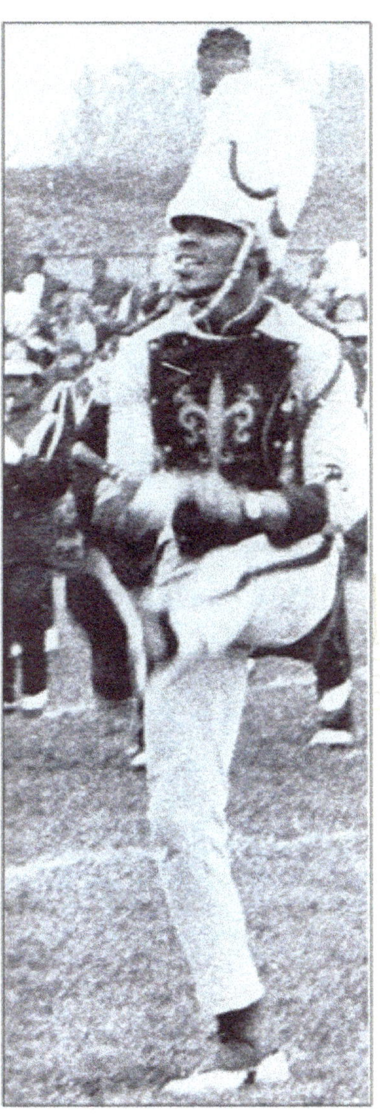

Virginia State Collage, Marching 110, Half-Time Show, Perry "Rusty" Chamblis, Petersburg, Virginia, "Rusty doing his thing!". 1971.

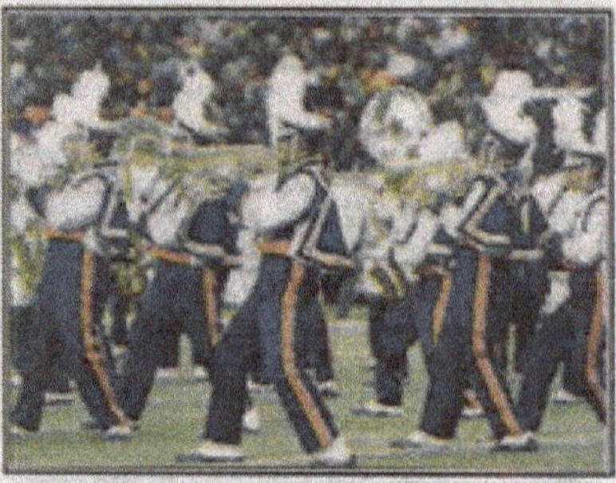

VSU Among 8 HBCU's For Honda Battle of The Bands Showcase

TORRANCE, CA

Virginia State University has emerged as one of the top eight HBCU marching bands selected to perform at the 2011 Honda Battle of the Bands Invitational Showcase. The event will take place on January 29th at the Georgia Dome in Atlanta.

The journey of 45 Historically Black College and University (HBCU) Marching Bands began in late summer when these HBCU's took the first high step and first rehearsal where increasingly challenging drills and compositions were tested to develop the most dynamic, spirited halftime performances of the fall season.

This is the eighth year the "Marching Trojan Explosion" from the Central Intercollegiate Athletic Association has been selected. Honda has been sponsoring the competition for nine years. VSU will be competing against the HBCU's that follow.

• South Carolina State University "Marching 101" (Mid-Eastern Athletic Conference)

• Albany State University "Marching Rams Show Band" (Southern Intercollegiate Athletic Conference)

• Jackson State University "Sonic Boom of the South" (Southwestern Athletic Conference)

• Bethune-Cookman University "Marching Wildcats" (Mid-Eastern Athletic Conference)

• Clark Atlanta University "Mighty Marching Panthers" (Southern Intercollegiate Athletic Conference)

• Winston-Salem State University "Red Sea of Sound" (Central Intercollegiate Athletic Association)

• Tennessee State University "Aristocrat of Bands" (Ohio Valley Conference)

The 2,000 student-musicians that make up these bands have staked their claims to being among the elite in the country. Each band will have the opportunity to perform for 12 minutes and showcase their musical skills, dancing talents and creativity. This year's showcase features first-time South Carolina State University as well as eight-time participant Virginia State University. Band sizes range from the small but powerful 120-member ensemble of Clark Atlanta University, to the 400-member goliath of Bethune-Cookman.

Marking its ninth year, the Honda Battle of the Bands is the only national scholarship program that highlights music education as an important facet of HBCU heritage and culture. The eight winning band programs chosen to participate in this year's Invitational Showcase will be awarded $20,000 by American Honda for their music programs, in addition to the $1,000 grant they received for participation in the pre-qualifying Celebration Tour.

Through this program, American Honda annually awards a total of $205,000 in scholarships to HBCU music programs. Since the program's inception, an excess of $1 million in grant money has been bestowed to black colleges.

"The Honda Battle of the Bands Invitational Showcase is about more than what happens on the field at the Georgia Dome on show day," said Marc Burt, Senior Manager, Office of Inclusion and Diversity for American Honda. "This event is about celebrating the abilities and brilliance of young people coming out of the nation's black colleges. The discipline and drive these student-musicians exhibit both on and off the field are phenomenal, and Honda is pleased to be able to contribute to the music education programs that help foster the artistic and academic growth of these students."

Group and individual tickets to this highly anticipated family event are on sale now and can be purchased for $10-to-$12 by visiting www.HondaBattleoftheBands.com, through Ticketmaster or via the Georgia Dome box-office.

For more information about the program, please visit www.HondaBattleoftheBands.com.

V S U Among 8 HBCU's For Honda Battle of Bands Invitational Showcase in Atlanta, Georgia, "Preparing for competition at the Georgia Dome!", Circa 2003.

NOTEWORTHY MILESTONES

• Claiborne Richardson did not return as band director at Virginia State in 1973.

• Oneil Sanford came on board as Virginia State's band director in 1973.

• S. H. Clarke Junior High School continues as its new designation of Steven H. Clarke Academy.

• Cradock High School discontinued operation in 1990.

• Virginia State College transitions to Virginia State University in 1980.

• • •

• Emery Fears, legendary high school band director, moves from the I. C. Norcom High School Greyhounds in Portsmouth, VA, and becomes director of bands at Norfolk State University, marking the beginning of the Spartan "legion" marching band.

• Legendary VSU Marching 110 band changes name to Marching Trojan Explosion band circa 1980.

• VSU drumline, Orange Crush performed a second time for President Barack Obama at the Siegle Center in Richmond, VA, as he announced his intentions to run for a second term as president of the United States.

"Director of bands, Dr. Mark W. Phillips, VSU homecoming, October 20, 2012.

• VSU "Orange Crush drumline ranked third in the country among all marching bands.

"Dr. Mark W. Phillips, director of bands,
VSU homecoming, October 20, 2012. See: "bleacher report"

Trussell, the VSU soul, rock, funk band changes name to "Mass Production," circa: late 1970s/early 1980.

"The name VSU Marching 110 band went as far back as to 1960…

The VSU Marching 110 band regularly performed during National

Football League half-time shows for the Washington Redskins at RFK Stadium in Washington, D.C.; the Baltimore Colts at Memorial Stadium in Baltimore, MD; for the New York Giants at Yankee Stadium in the Bronx, NYC; for the Pittsburgh Steelers at Three Rivers Stadium in Pittsburgh, PA; and the Philadelphia Eagles at their stadium prior to Veterans Stadium."

"Mr. Starrie Jordan, October 12, 2013.
VSU Marching 110, bass horn player, 1961.

• • •

In 1980, VSU's soul, rock, funk band, Trussell, got national air time with their hit recording of "Love Injection." "Love Injection" received frequent air time on the national syndicated televised show "Soul Train. It was regularly played as the background music for the soul train line and the soul train scramble board.

One Soul Train episode, I remember was when Soul Train dancer Jeffery Daniels and his all male dance troupe introduced and demonstrated to a national audience the new dance crave known as "poping and locking."

During the presentation, it was the first time that audiences got a chance to witness still another new dance called the "moon walk" with Trussell's "Love Injection" as it's back beat. "Love Injection" had a Caribbean, calypso, funk type of sound, undoubtedly derived from the back beat funk rhythms of the Marching 110 and its drum section and the various Marching 110 horn and guitar sections, which the majority of Trussell's/Mass Production's members had their professional beginnings in organized bandmanship.

• • •

December 1, 2018: Virginia State University's Trojan explosion marching band was invited to perform and performed in the 2018 Cox Communication Christmas Holiday Parade in Virginia Beach, VA. This was the Trojan Explosion's first performance of marching in the city's holiday Christmas parade.

• • •

News bulletin 2017: Washington Redskins, Training Camp
Fan Appreciation Day
Featuring the Virginia State University
Trojan Explosion Marching Band
12:00 P.M. Performance Time

VSU Alumni Association e-newsletter August 4, 2017
Washington Redskins, 85 years
Saturday, August 5, 2017, Richmond, VA
Training Camp
Fan Appreciation Day
Featuring the
Virginia State University
Trojan Explosion Marching Band
12:00 P.M. Performance Time

Bandmember Appreciation

Virginia communities represented by marching and concert band members:

S. H. Clarke Junior High School, Portsmouth, VA

Truxtun, Douglas Park, Maplewood Park, Brighton, Lincoln Park, Ida Barbour Homes, Jeffrey Wilson Homes, Prentis Park, Park View, Swanson Homes, Norcom Park, Mount Herman, Washington Park, Dales Homes, Newtown, and Prentis Place;

Cradock High School, Portsmouth, VA

Truxtun, Highland Biltmore, Stanley Court, Academy Park, the town of Cradock Cavalier Manor, Victory Manor, Newtown, Prentis Park, Maplewood Park, and Brighton;

Virginia State College, Petersburg, VA

Portsmouth, Norfolk, Virginia Beach, Chesapeake, Hampton, Newport News, Williamsburg, Ettrick, Petersburg, Richmond, Charlottesville, Louisa, Bowling Green, Tappahannock, Crewe, Lynchburg, Roanoke, Goochland, King William, Buckingham,

Saluda, Dinwiddie, Suffolk, Courtland, Jarratt, Emporia, South Hill, Chase City, South Boston, Danville, Martinsville, Waverly, Smithfield, New Kent, King and Queen County, Chattem, Pocahontas, Charles City, Farmville, Hopewell, Northumberland, Powatan, and Colonial Heights.

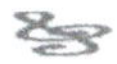

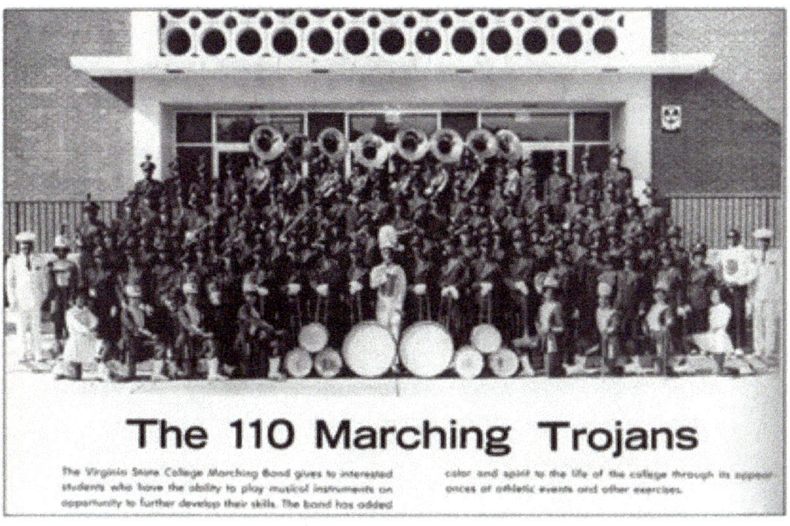

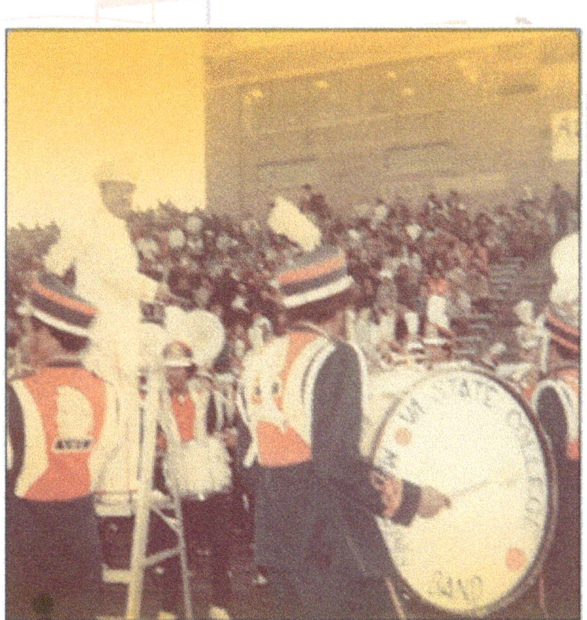

Virginia State College Marching 110, Rogers Stadium, Petersburg, Virginia, "Center Snare drummer in front of the ladder is yours truly!"; "Mr. Claiborne "Stix" Richardson, VSC Band Director on ladder!"; "Calvin Powell is steady on the Bass Drum!", 1971.

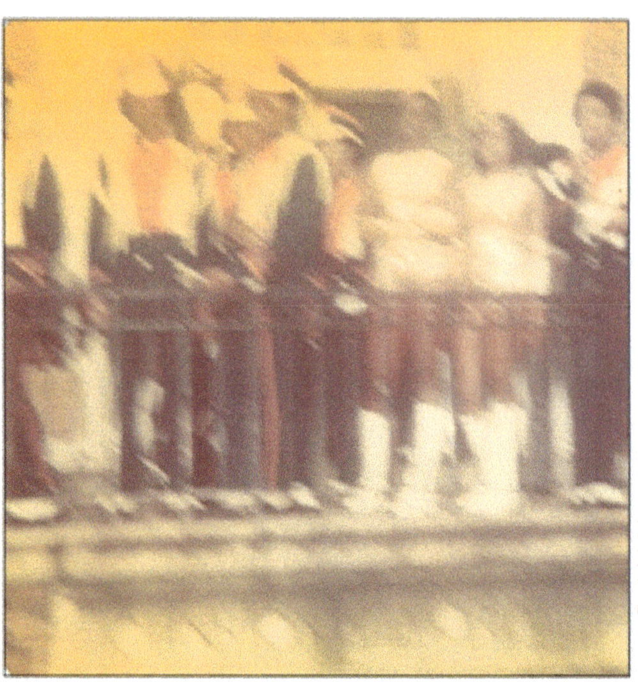

Virginia State College Marching 110 Band members standing on the steps in front the music building upon returning from the stadium, Petersburg, Virginia, "I dont't known if this one will be a go? Kind of foggy!", 1971.

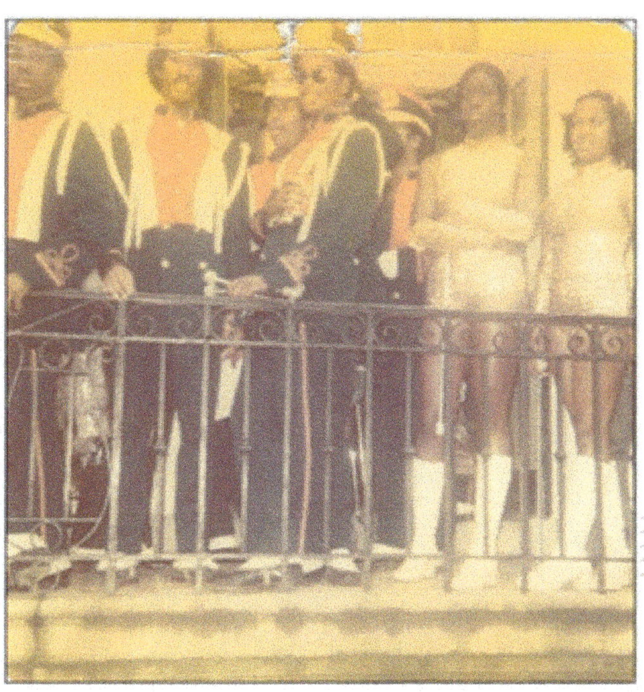

Virginia State College Marching 110 Band members standing on the steps in front the music building upon returning from the stadium performance & after the drum section's performance at the music building. "Yours truly in the center with drum straps; Nat Lee with sunglasses and tenor mallots along with the " Golden Girls"!", Petersburg, Virginia, 1971.

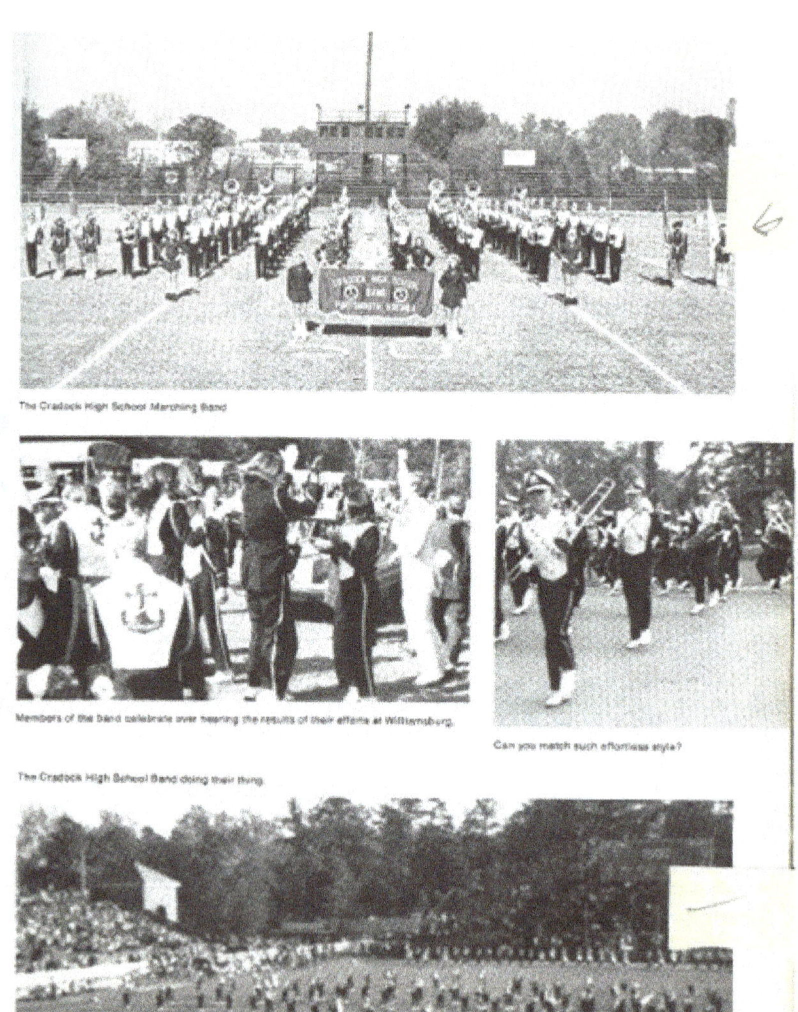

Cradock High School Marching Band, Portsmouth, Virginia, Admiral's Stadium along with the bands excitement of the results of competing at the State Championship at The College of William & Mary in Williamsburg, Virginia, "We placed 2nd in the State!", 1971

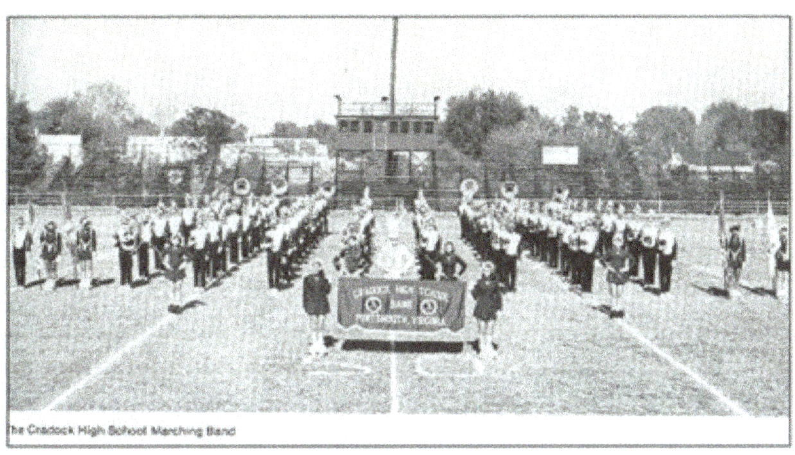

Cradock High School Marching Band at home in Admiral's Stadium, 1971.

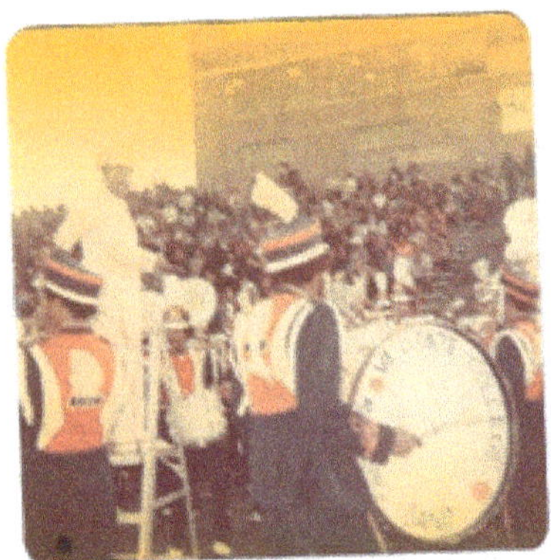

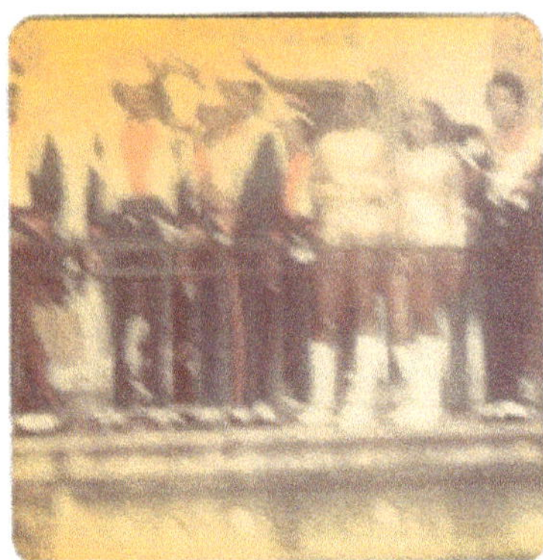

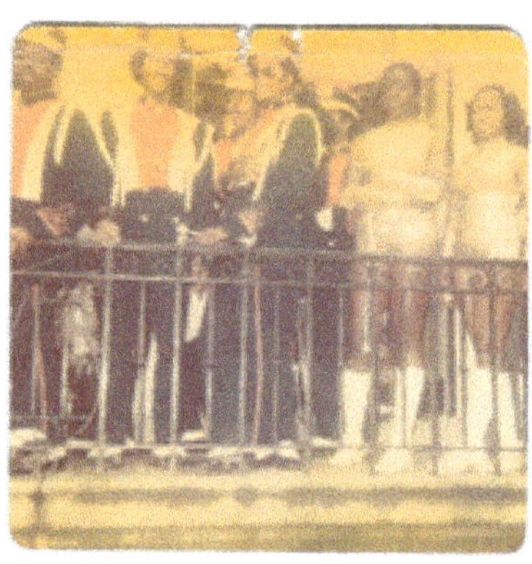

Virginia State College , collage collection; "MR. Claiborne "Stix' Richardson, Band Director on ladder; yours truly is snare drummer in front of ladder; Calvin Powell, always steady on Bass Drum; Band members on steps of music building after successful performance by the Marching 110 with the "Golden Girls" & drum section performance; Nat Lee with tenor mallots & sunglasses!", 1971.

PERCUSSIVE ARTS SOCIETY INTERNATIONAL DRUM RUDIMENTS

All rudiments should be practiced: open (slow) to close (fast) to open (slow) and/or at an even moderate march tempo.

I. ROLL RUDIMENTS

NEXT PAGE

A. Single Stroke Roll Rudiments

1. SINGLE STROKE ROLL *

2. SINGLE STROKE FOUR

3. SINGLE STROKE SEVEN

B. MULTIPLE BOUNCE ROLL RUDIMENTS

4. MULTIPLE BOUNCE ROLL

5. TRIPLE STROKE ROLL

C. DOUBLE STROKE OPEN ROLL RUDIMENTS

6. DOUBLE STROKE OPEN ROLL *

7. FIVE STROKE ROLL

8. SIX STROKE ROLL

9. SEVEN STROKE ROLL *

10. NINE STROKE ROLL *

11. TEN STROKE ROLL *

12. ELEVEN STROKE ROLL *

13. THIRTEEN STROKE ROLL *

14. FIFTEEN STROKE ROLL

15. SEVENTEEN STROKE ROLL

II. DIDDLE RUDIMENTS

16. SINGLE PARADIDDLE *

17. DOUBLE PARADIDDLE *

18. TRIPLE PARADIDDLE

19. SINGLE PARADIDDLE-DIDDLE

* These rudiments are also included in the original Standard 26 American Drum Rudiments

Standard Snare Drum Rudiments.

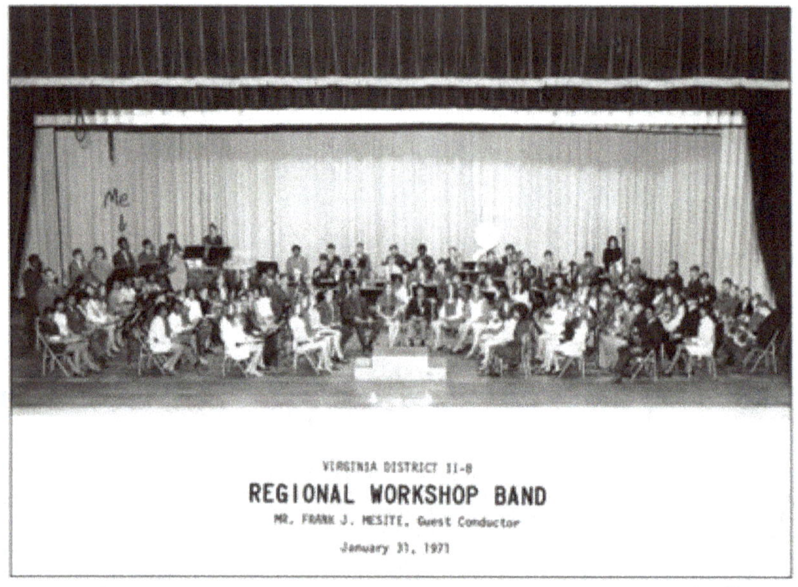

Cradock High School Auditorium, Portsmouth, Virginia District II-B. Mr. Frank J. Mesite, Guest Conductor, January, 1971.

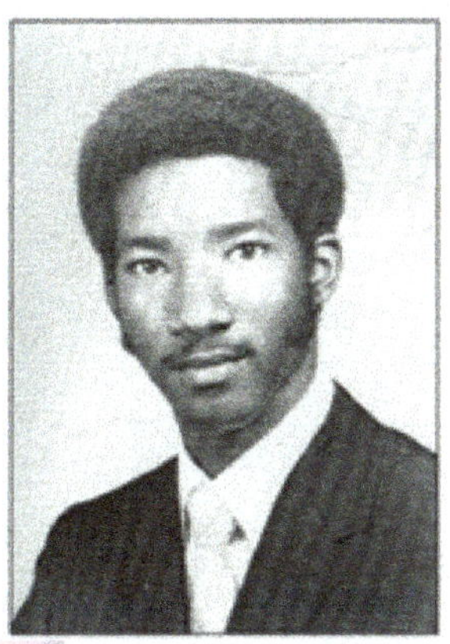

Cradock High School, Portsmouth, Virginia, "Yours truly, Senior Photo, The Afro was coming!", 1971.

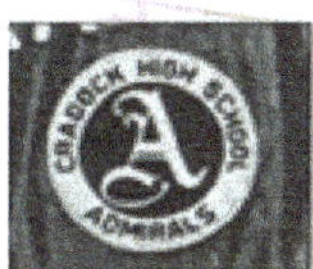

Cradock High School, Portsmouth, Virginia, Admirals Logo, 1971

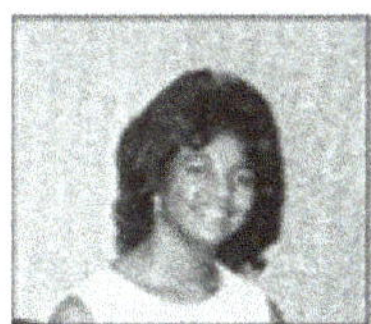

Cradock High School, Portsmouth, Virginia, Mrs. Jerlene Harding, Orchestra Director, "Simply the best!", 1971.

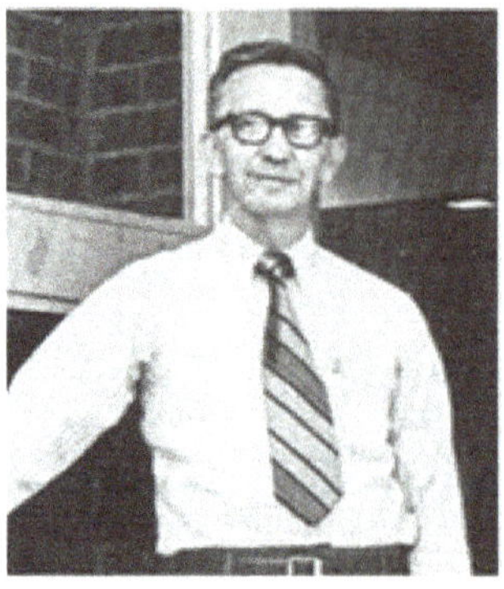

Cradock High School, Portsmouth, Virginia, Mr. William P. Barley, Band Director, "Standing in the band room doorway; Set positive tone for the races and his band!", 1971.

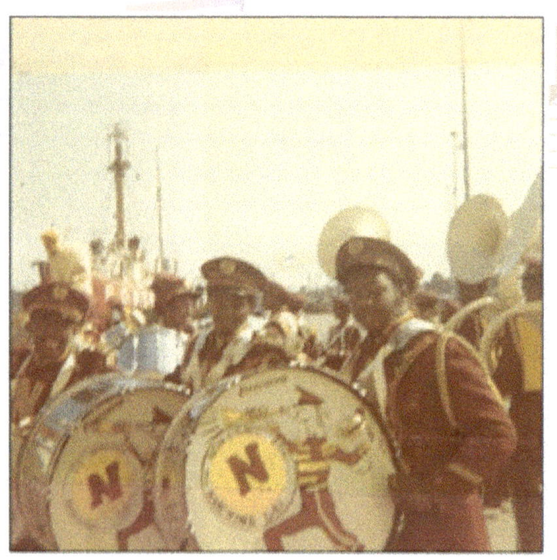

I.C. Norcom High School Marching Greyhounds, Portsmouth, Virginia. "Drummers and friends, James Weston on Tenor Drum & Wayne White, Bass-Drum center, Clifton Haynes, Bass-Drum right with Fiberglass Bass Horns in the background right; Preparing to line-up at the foot of High Street for the Oyster Bowl Parade!" "Love the Marching Greyhounds drum-hide art work!", 1971.

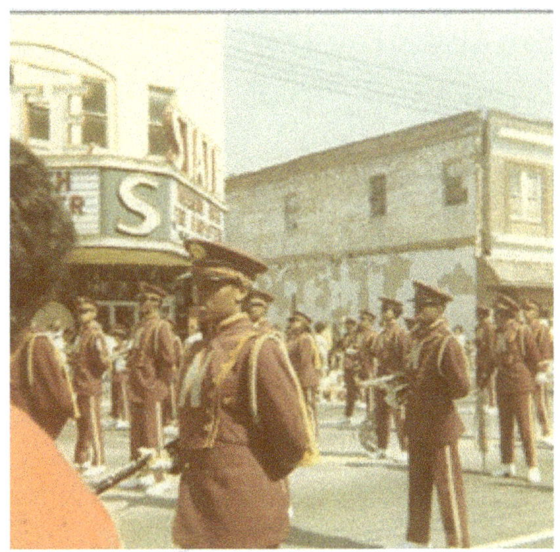

I.C Norcom High School Marching Greyhounds, High Street, Portsmouth, Virginia oyster Bowl Parare; "At ease with great discipline", 1971.

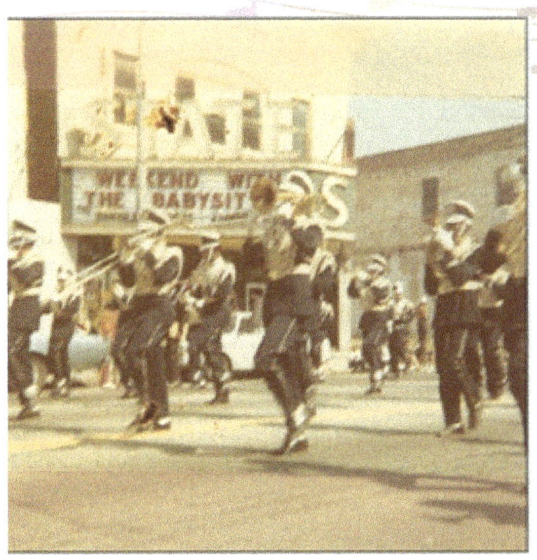

Norfolk State College Marching Band, High Street, Portsmouth, Virginia, Oyster Bowl Parade; "In Blue uniforms with front line stepping it out!", 1971.

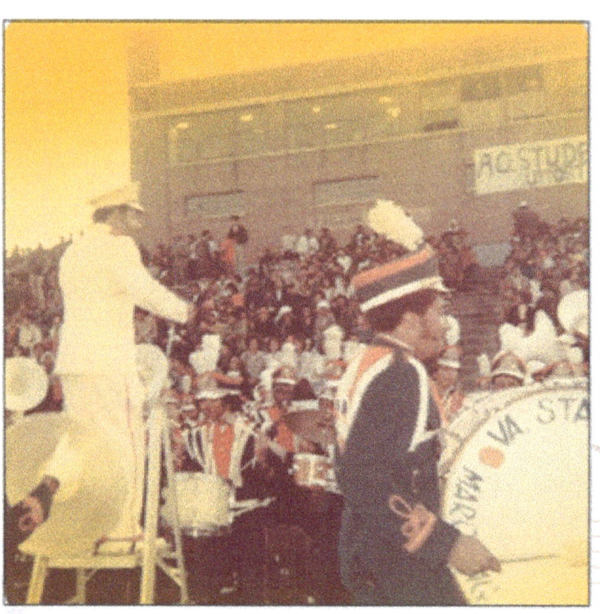

Virginia State College Marching 110 drum section after half-time show, Rogers Stadium. "Mr. Claiborne "Stix" Richardson on ladder; Yours truly on snare drum in front of ladder; Calvin Powell on Baase Drum; Marching 110 prepares to rock the stadium!", 1971.

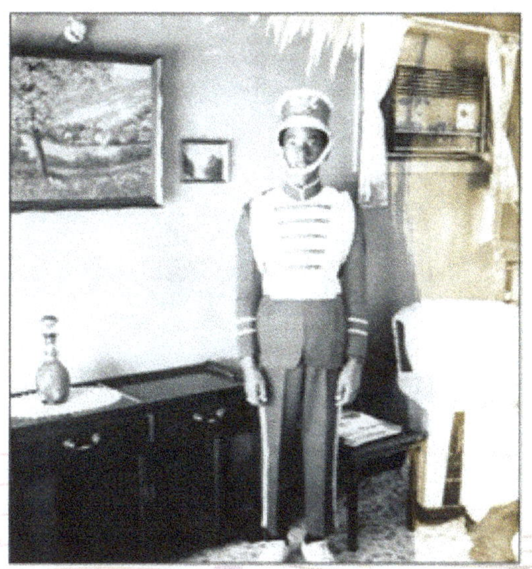

Yours truly; S. H. Clarke Junior High School, Portsmouth, Virginia, marching band uniform, "In my home where it all began!", 1965.

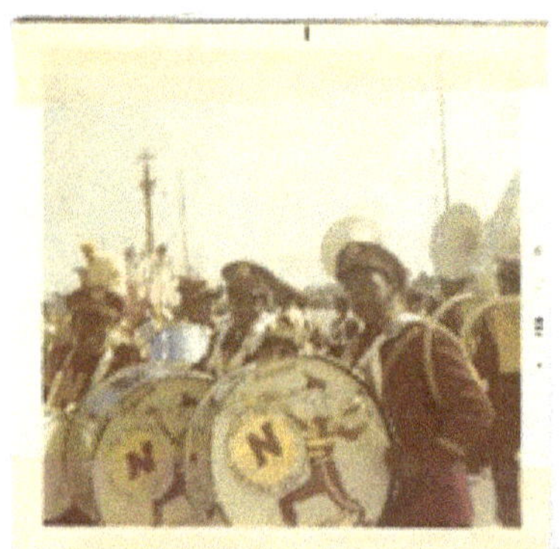

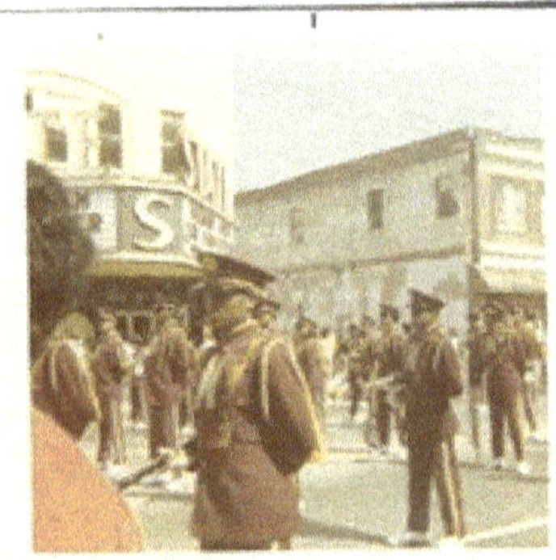

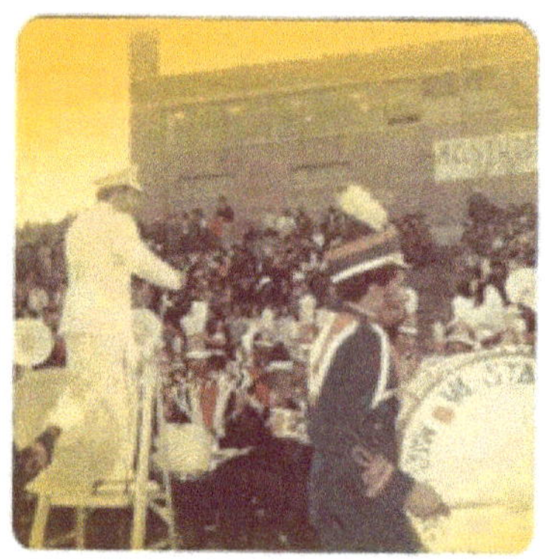

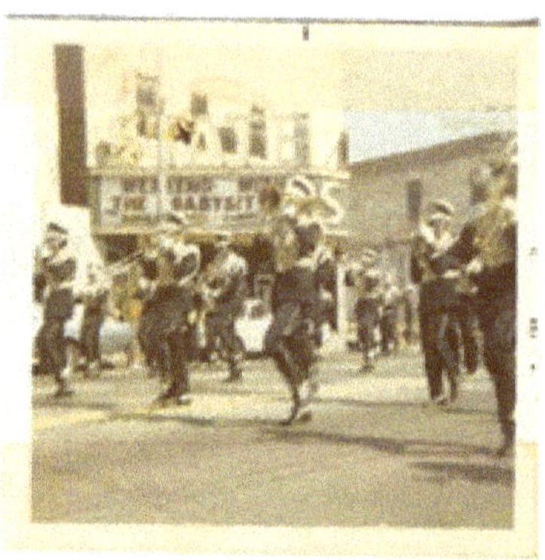

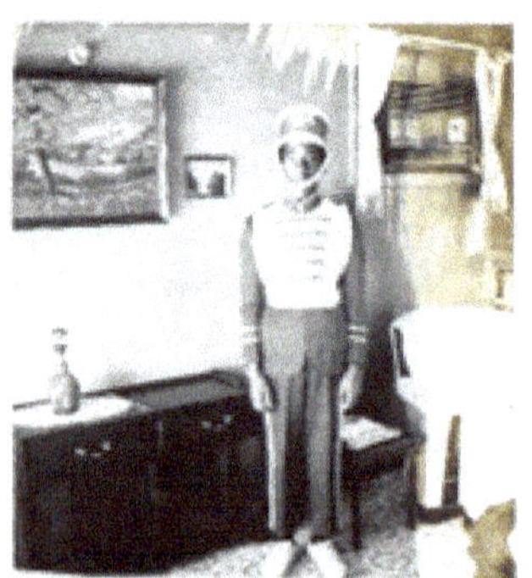

"Photo collage, I.C. Norcom Marching Greyhounds; Norfolk State College marching band; yours truly in Junior High School marching band uniform at home!"

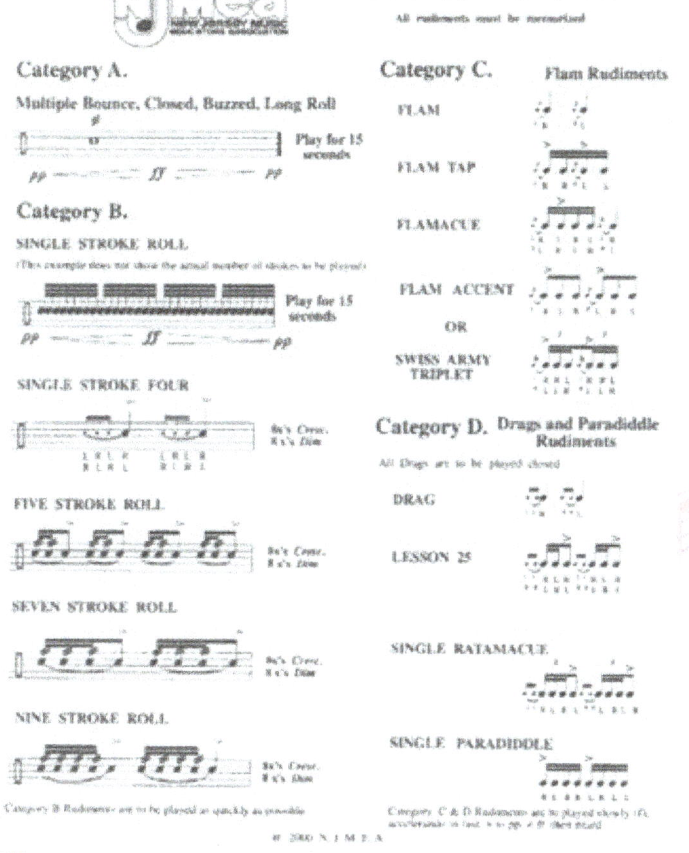

"Single Stroke Roll leads if off!"

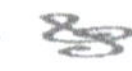

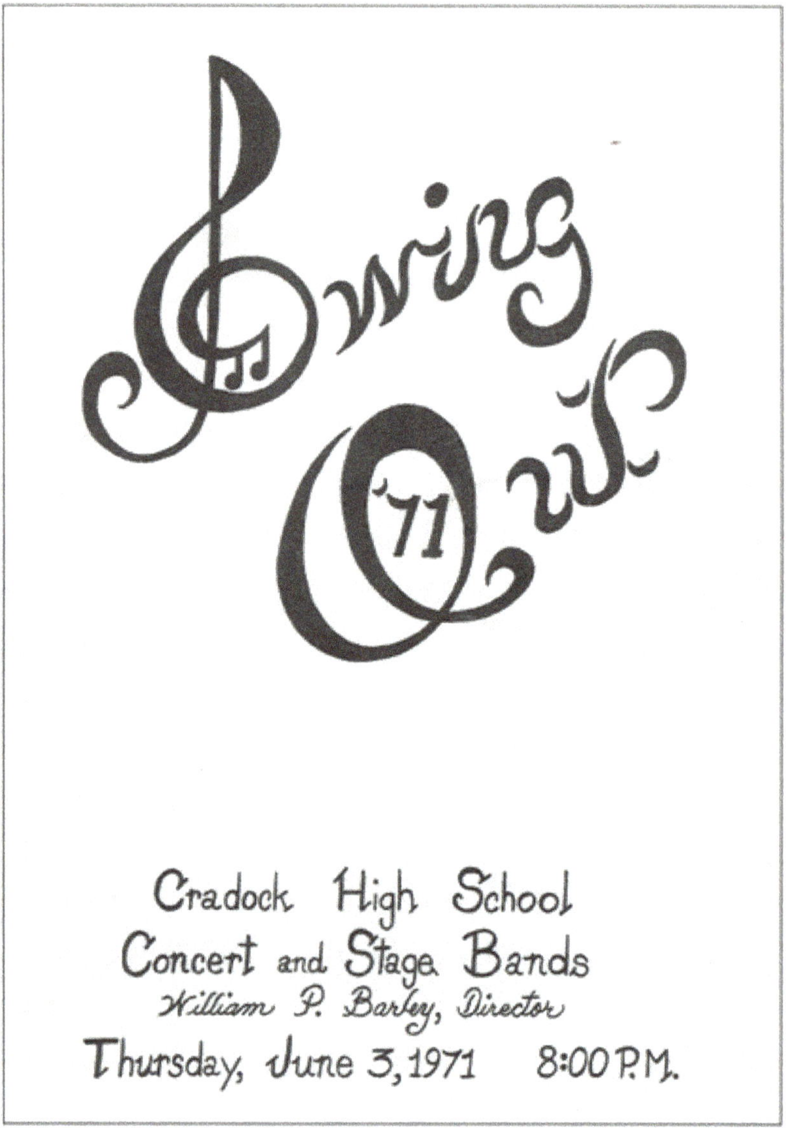

Cradock High School, Portsmouth, Virginia; Concert and Stage Bands; William P. Barley, Director; June 1971.

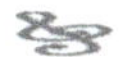

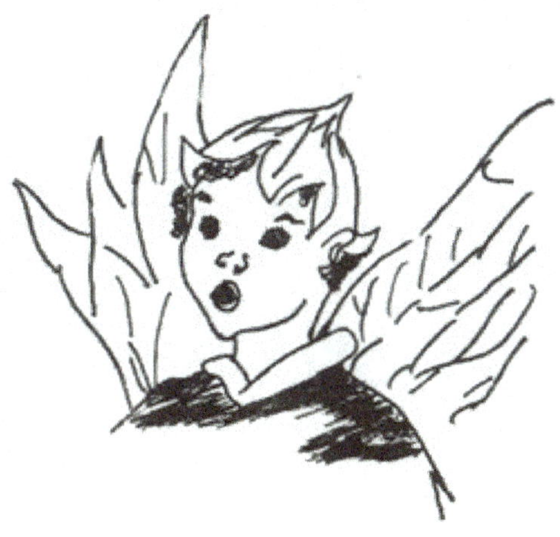

Cradock High School, Portsmouth, Virginia; Orchestra Choir Spring Concert; Mrs. Jerlene Harding, Orchestra Conductor; Mre.s Harriet Heath, Choral DIrector; May, 1971.

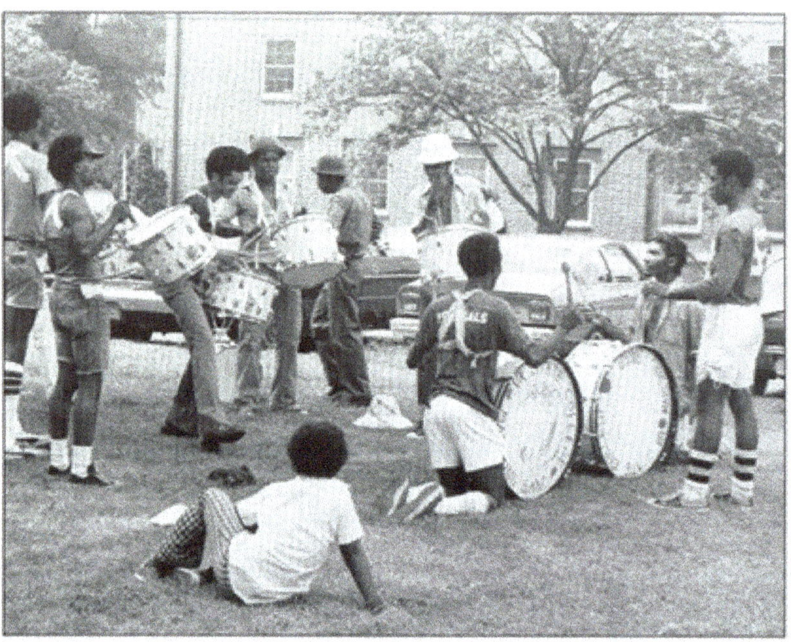

Virginia State Collage, Petersburg, Virginia. "Drum section strapped-up, practicing among themselves. Notice the Pearl Snare, Tenor and Bass drums!", 1974.

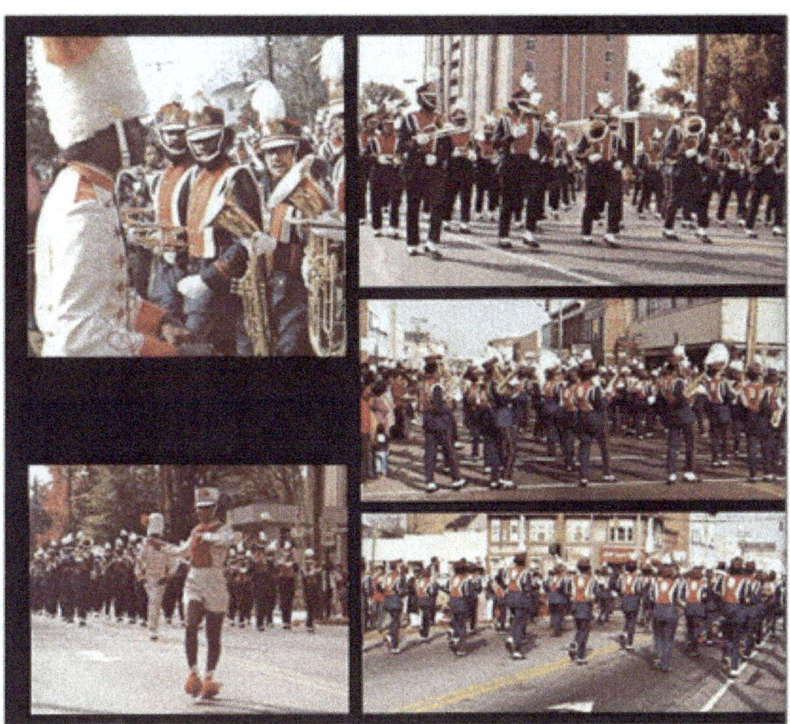

Photo Collage, "Virginia State College Marching 110 marching in the
Homecoming Parade, Downtown Petersburg, Virginia!", 1974.

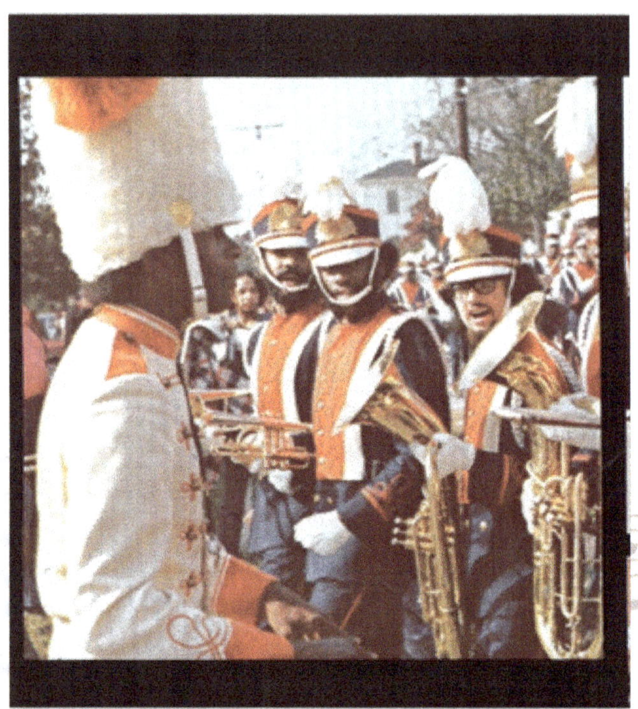

"Virginia State College Drum Major pumping-up the brass section with a pep-talk before stepping-off for the Homecoming Parade, Downtown Petersburg, Virginia!", 1974.

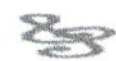

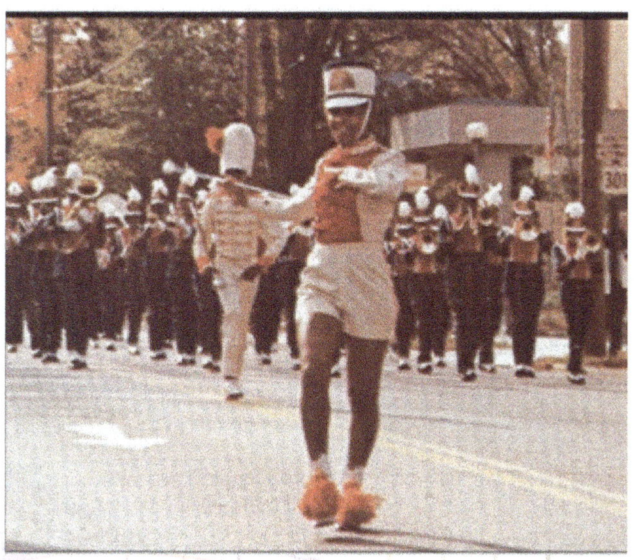

"Virginia State College Marjorette strutting her stuff, Homecoming Parade Downtown Petersburg, Virginia!", 1974.

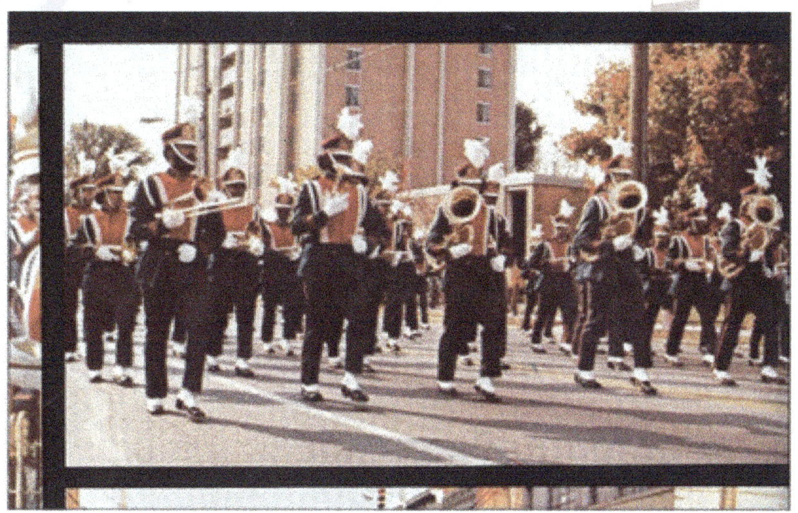

"Virginia State College Marching 110 front-line setting the tone, Homecoming Parade, Downtown, Petersburg, Virginia", 1974.

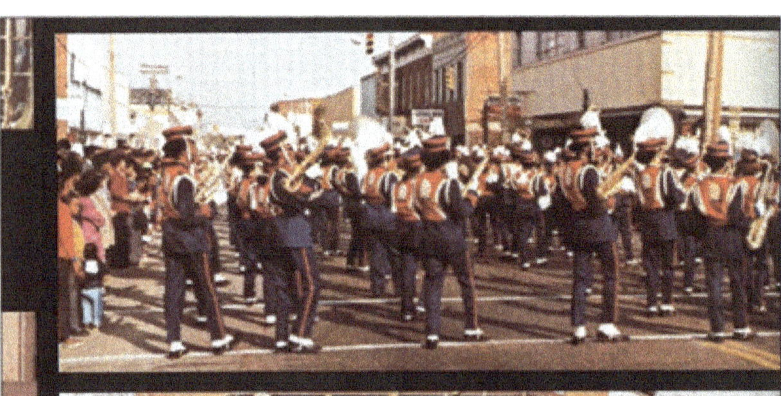

"Virginia State College Marching 110 makes that left-turn onto Sycamore Street, Downtown Petersburg, Virginia as the crowd anticipates their arrival!", 1974.

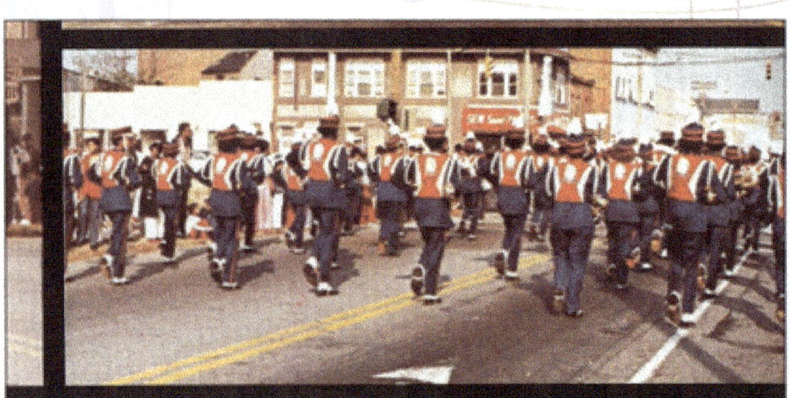

"Virginia State College Marching 110, Homecoming Parade, Downtown Petersburg, Virginia; notice the alignment while moving!", 1974.

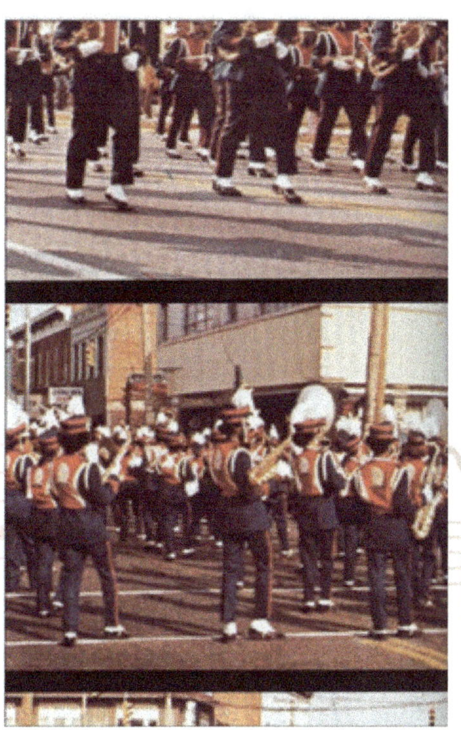

"Virginia State College Marching 110 makes the left-turn onto Sycamore Street, in slow motion, Downtown Petersburg, Viginia!", 1974.

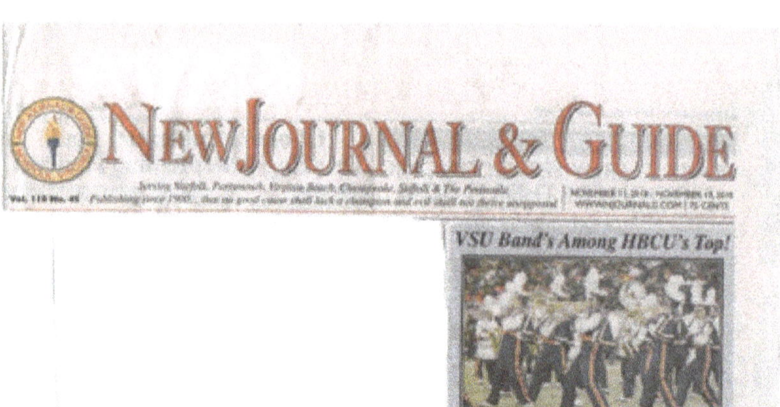

VSU Bands Among HBCU's Top!; News Article, New Journal Guid, www.thenewjournalandguide.com; "8th straight year for "Trojan Explosion" marching band!", January 2011.

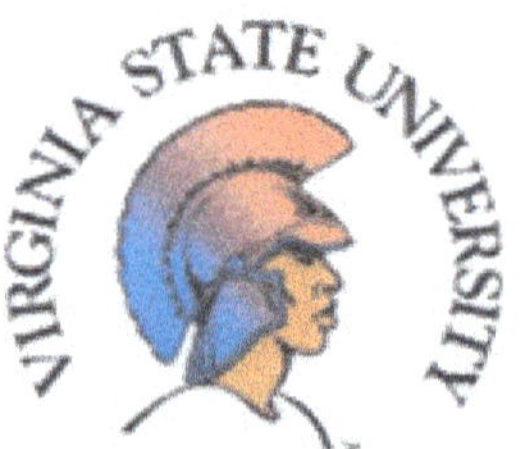

Trojan Logo

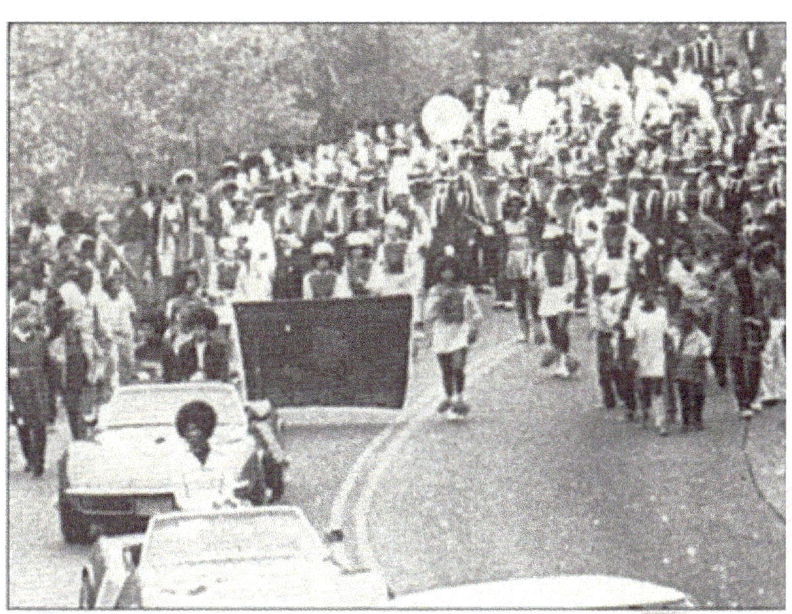

"Virginia State College Marching 110 advances in Homecoming Parade with Corvette's leading the processional as the crowd on the parade route clamors in excitement; Petersburg, Virginia!", Circa, 1971.

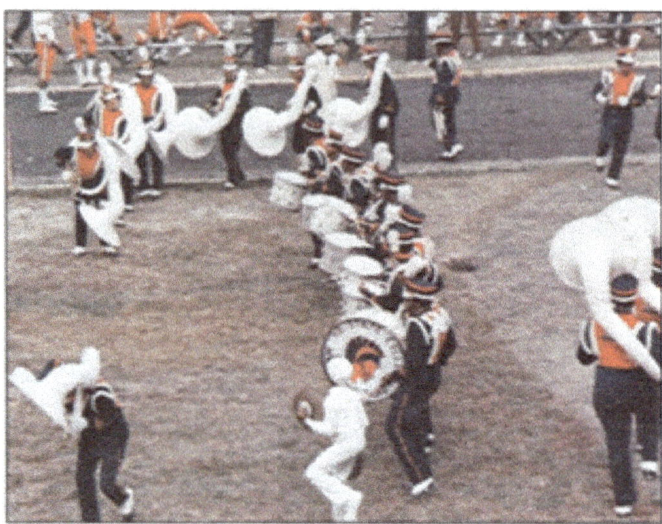

Ariel view as Virginia State College Marching 110 drum section form a lane for bass horn players, with their all white fiberglass bass horns, 10 of them, one has already gone through the lane, to start their show moving into the stands after the half-time show; Calvin Powell on Bass Drum and Young Claiborne in all white on cymbals with Mr. Richardson on the track in all white directors uniform directing the scene; Notice also the bass drum hide's Trojan art work!", 1971.

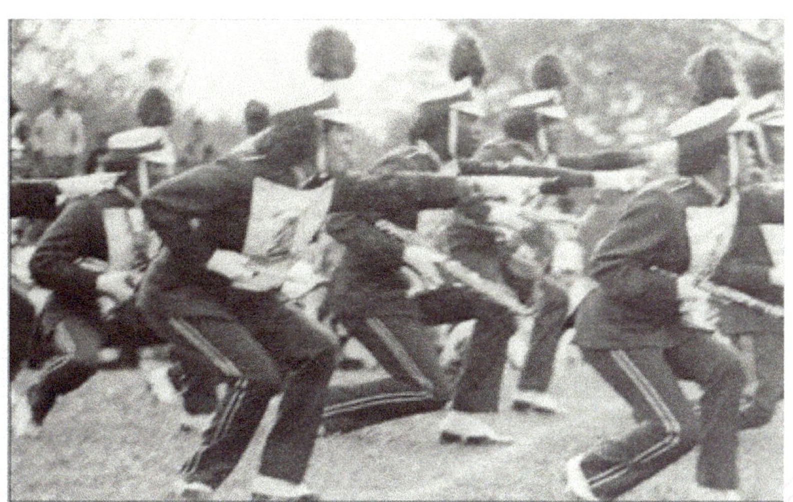

VSU 75

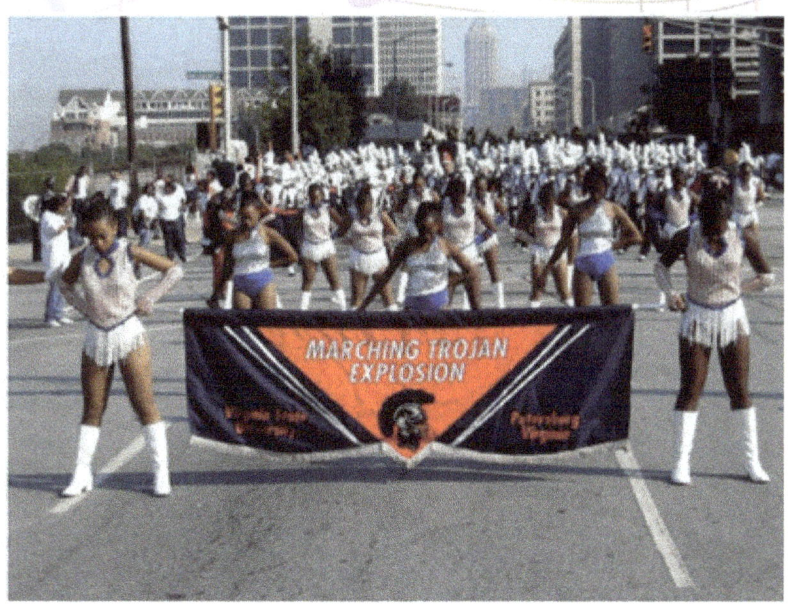

VSU 2003

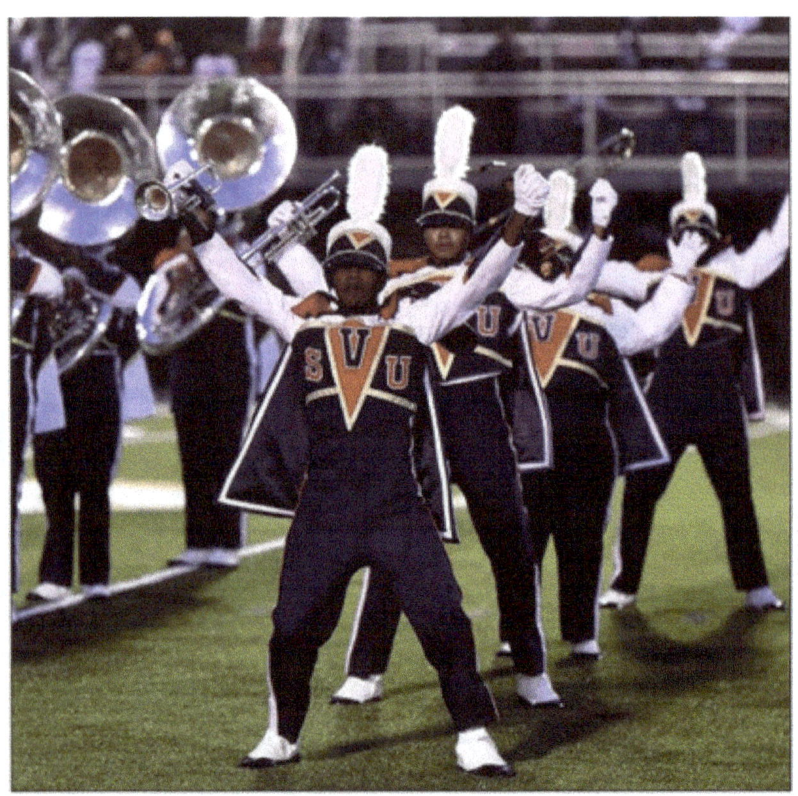

VSU Current

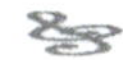

DRUMLINE HONOR ROLL

S. H. Clarke Junior High School

James Weston
Donald Boston
Jimmy Flyte
Fred Collins
Richard Cansel
William "Billy" Richardson
Timothy Casey
Wayne White
Bobby Earl Dunn
Jack Howell

Cradock High School

Teddy Greene
Richard Cansel
Robert "Bobby" Wilbourn
Roger Moncovich
Herby Coleman
Shelton Mutter
Terry Riffe
Janet Wilson
Loretta Land
Rickey Lawrence
George Mickley
Charles Jordan
Steve Morris
Albert Sykes

Virginia State College

Mike Thrift
Calvin Powell
Julius Dyson

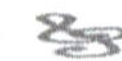

Ron Smith
Nat Lee
Young Claiborne Richardson, Jr.
Robert Kemp
Robert McDonald
Edward Thornton
Randolph C. Harrison
Hollis "Moose" Morris
Kevin Curtis
Bernard Hardy

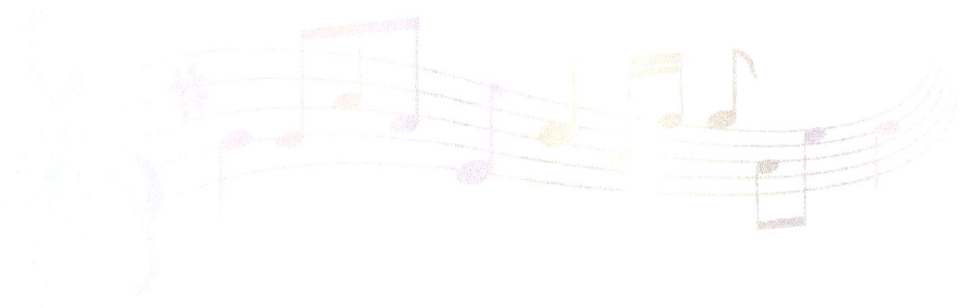

EMAILS

Date: October 1, 2007

Subj: "The Return of the Marching 110" in Honor of the VSU Trojan Explosion Alumni Band

That's right, your VSU alumni band will be in full swing this year at the 2007 homecoming. We are calling on all alumni band members to come out and participate. Two pre-practices will be held at Davis Hall on the campus of VSU. Mr. Harold J. Haughton, Sr., "King of Marching Bands," will be conducting the alumni band. Dress for homecoming is navy sweat pants and white sneakers…cost is $30, which covers your shirt, ticket, and donation to the band.

(For those that don't know, the Marching 110 was the name of the band prior to the Trojan Explosion) :)

Alumni Band Committee:
Harold J. Haughton, Sr. (Director of Alumni Band)
Maurice H. Bowles III (VSU Band Staff)
Salena Scott (VSU Band Staff/Dancers)
L. Darnell Spicely (VSU Band Staff)

Date: Sunday, February 21, 2010

Fr: VSU Alumni Band

Subj: VSU Drumline Headed to D.C. to Play for President Obama

The Virginia State University drumline "Orange Thunder" has been selected to perform in D.C. this upcoming Friday for the signing of the HBCU funding bill that will be signed by the president…

The VSU Trojan Explosion marching band got a lot of recognition from being a seven-time repeat participant in the Honda Battle of the Bands in Atlanta, which put the band in the spotlight of success to be selected…

Congrats to percussion instructor Elijah Powell and the entire VSU band family on this monumental moment…

Musically yours,
VSU Band Staff and Alumni Band Members
Virginia State University Alumni Association

Date: Saturday, February 27, 2010

Subj: VSU Makes History at the White House

Great news! Virginia State University's Trojan Explosion marching band made history yesterday (Friday, February 26) by performing at the White House…Members of the band's drumline known affectionally as "Orange Thunder" entertained those who were in the audience to see President Barack Obama sign an executive order recognizing the nation's 105 Historically Black Colleges and Universities. Dr. Mark Phillips, VSU Band Director and Elijah Powell, drum instructor, were also on hand to witness this event…

During opening remarks, the President noted that he believed the presence of the Trojan Explosion drumline marked the first time there's been a drumline in the White House…

Date: Sunday, February 28, 2010

Fr: Elania Jemison Hudson

Subj: VSUAA online connection video: vsu drumline @ the white house "A nine-person drumline from Virginia State University plays in cross hall of the White House before an event honoring historically black colleges and universities, February 26, 2010…

Video can be viewed at: http://youtube.com/watch?v=akpuhrcilqa

Milestone
News Bulletin 2017: Washington Redskins, TRAINING CAMP
Fan Appreciation Day
Featuring the Virginia State University
Trojan Explosion Marching Band
12:00 P.M. Performance Time

VSU Alumni Association E-Newsletter August 4, 2017
 WASHINGTON REDSKINS, 85 Years

Saturday, August 5, 2017, Richmond, VA
TRAINING CAMP
Fan Appreciation Day
Featuring the
Virginia State University
Trojan Explosion Marching Band
12:00 P.M. Performance Time

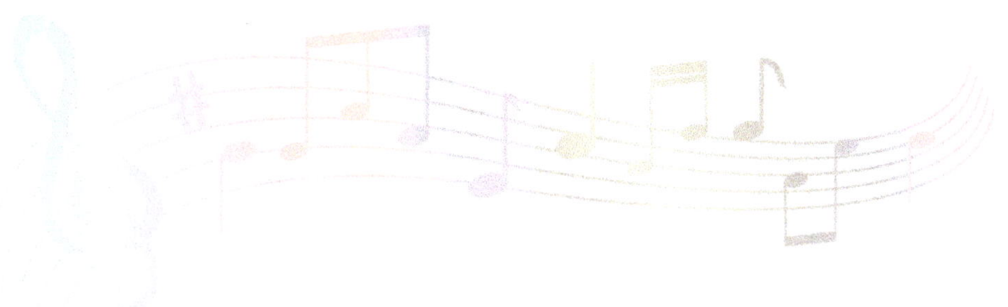

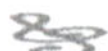

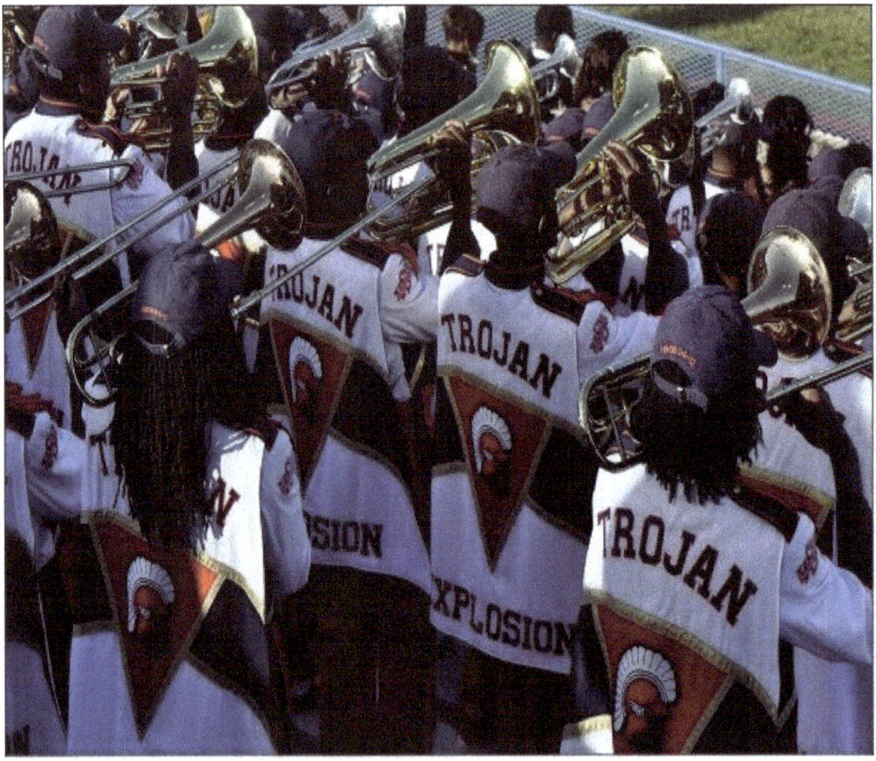

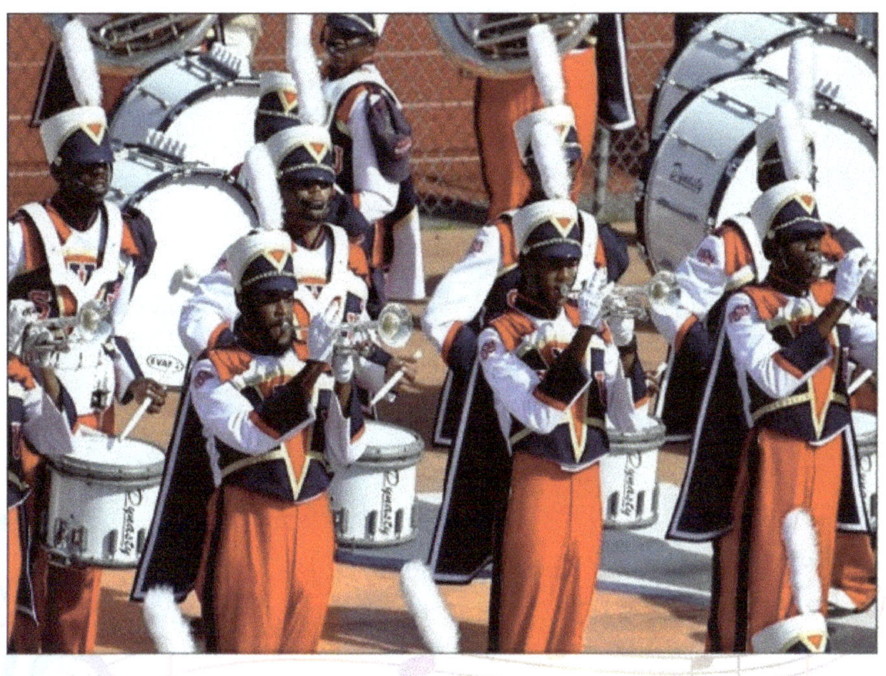

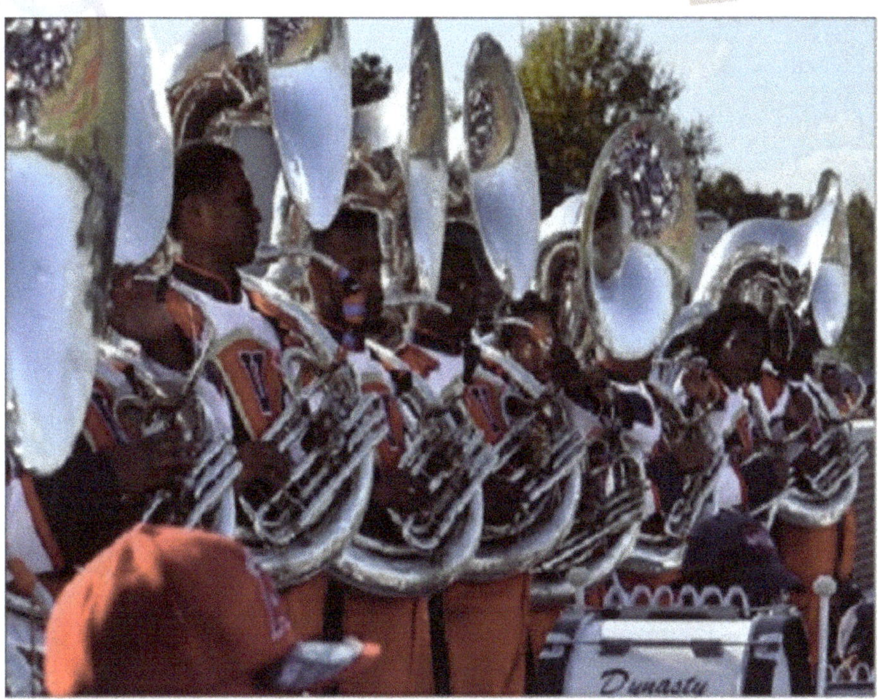

EPILOGUE

Hilda Cooper, Drum Majorette, Booker T. Washington High School, Rocky Mount, NC, 1958-1965

From 1954 to 1958, Hilda was in elementary school. Prior to 1958, all grades attended the same school from elementary through high school. In North Carolina, all schools were segregated until 1967. Booker T. Washington's school motto was "Be Somebody," and the school colors were blue and gold.

The drum majorette was the head majorette. I was marching in the band beginning in kindergarten through high school.

The drum majorette stood alone in front of the band, as the drum major does. Majorettes had to posture themselves in the high stepping position with legs up and toes pointed to the ground, and step. We were able to stand on one leg with our toes pointed with the other leg. There was no wiggling or wobbling.

Majorettes had to twirl the baton through their fingers while marching and bring it around behind your back.

I enjoyed the bass drum. My cousin played the bass drum and another cousin played the drums.

Just the rhythm of it gets me moving…I can hear it on T.V. and it gets me moving.

I loved it when the band traveled to places to perform. We would be clean!

We were precise with grace. You couldn't be out of line. There were no sneakers but black shoes with spats.

…Those were the good 'ole days!

Velvoria Beamon Carey, Majorette, I. C. Norcom High School Greyhounds, Portsmouth, VA, early 1960s

Velvoria expressed that she felt that being a majorette wasn't strenuous during her time. They would come home from school and really go through a hard workout in the street in front of the house.

Potential majorettes tried out for the position and auditioned one at a time. Each audition had to follow the protocol of high-step with toes pointed on one leg and thighs at a 45-degree angle, sort of on the scale of the collegiate majorette protocol.

The majorettes set the tone and the standard. You just had to keep the line straight. Majorette standard twirl routine included a figure-eight twirl, throw the baton in the air and catch it, followed by the backward twirl, and marching while twirling the baton.

The majorette's outfit included a fitted-type jacket, short skirt with boots, and a pom-pom tassel.

I asked Velvoria what she liked about the drum beat, and she said she liked the rhythm. "You've got to move."

Lastly, she leaned over toward me and whispered, "Also, the majorettes had to be light skin to medium light…No dark skin girls. Now, here in 2018, it's the very opposite. Most of the girls are dark skin… It has changed to the darker shade of hue."

Rose Stith Singleton, VSU Majorette Alumnus, 1972-1976, Homecoming 2018, October 21, 2018

It was night now at homecoming, and I saw Rose at the tailgate area just behind the Charles and Wanda Faye Taliaferro and Friends tailgate site. As she was moving about in that tent area, I approached her and asked her if she marched with the band today.

Most of the time when I see Rose, she has her majorette's baton with her. She replied, no, she didn't march this time. She continued, nowadays she just likes to have it in her hand. She snapped to a majorette's attention saying that she was ready to go.

I mentioned that someone has got to tell about what we did up here in the Marching 110 in the 1970s. She said that she agreed. Then she went on to talk about Rusty.

It had rained earlier that day of the homecoming, and there was a puddle of water just off to where we were standing.

She said, "Do you see that puddle over there?"

It had rained the day of band practice, and there was a puddle of mud on the practice field. Rusty had the band march through the puddle of mud. He stood there, watching, saying, "Do it again, do it again," until the mud was all over our clothes, up on our shirt collar… going through the mud puddle two or three times.

When you were muddy enough and didn't care about the conditions, Rusty said, "Now you're ready to practice."

Veronica Dungee Abrams, VSU Majorette Alumnus, 1969-1973, Town Hall Band Meeting, Homecoming 2018, October 21, 2018

Veronica and her husband, VSU alumnus Tony Abrams, arrived at the tailgate site of Charles and Wanda Faye Taliaferro and Friends and were greeting those gathered around the huge grill and Winnebago set-up. It was on the Friday evening of homecoming weekend as I had arrived in Petersburg and on campus early to make local visits of friends living in the Petersburg vicinity.

I approached Veronica, as I knew that she was a majorette in the Legendary Marching 110 band, asking her after we greeted each other, if she would be interested in going to the band meeting being held in the music building to discuss the future of the band. She talked with her husband and agreed to walk up to the music building with me to attend the meeting. Once again it found us making that long walk from the football stadium to the front campus area where the music building was located, not marching with the 110 this time.

As we walked up, I started talking about my freshman year having graduated from an integrated high school and playing in that band and getting to Virginia State that August just before the first football game. In the band room, Mr. Richardson announced that the band would be performing at Yankee Stadium at half-time for the Baltimore

Colts versus the New York Giants. I explained to her that I was in awe and wondered where I had come. Veronica said that she remembered that trip to New York City and mentioned an incident that she and another majorette were involved in at the YMCA where the band stayed overnight.

She recalled one of the majorette's going to the restroom where she saw a man's legs sticking out of one of the bathroom stalls and warned the other majorette's not to go in that rest room. The other majorette didn't go in that rest room, but it sure did freak both of them out to see that in a YMCA.

Then she said that she remembered when the band had a four-day weekend away from campus. The band left campus on Thursday for Pittsburgh to perform for the Steelers half-time, where she remembered it being "so cold." After Pittsburgh, it was on to New York to perform for the Giants at half-time and then traveling to the stadium where the Jets played and performing for half-time there.

The band returned to campus on Sunday night. Mr. Richardson gave each band member $10 for a food stipend, and her parents helped with some additional money.

Pam Cook, VSU Trojan Alumnus

November 10, 2018

This is my first time meeting Ms. Cook, who resides in Hampton Roads while sitting and chatting with the Alumni President, Laurie Carpenter after the Alumni meeting. I listened to Pam when excitement erupted in her voice as Laurie asked her about the Legendary Marching 110 band.

She explained that the drum major, Rusty, was the bomb. During half-time shows, the band would stretch from end-zone to end-zone, and Rusty would lead them onto the field. Once he got into his position on the 50-yard line, he would bend all the way backwards with the top of his drum major hat touching the ground. Oh, but when he came up with the drum major's baton, he would snap himself into a state of readiness and then it was on; everything was a go for the show to begin.

The band's sound would blow you back when you were sitting in the stands. I mean it would literally, you know, blow you back… (as she demonstrated by moving her head backwards). The band was a community onto itself.

When they would return for the practice field, mostly in the evenings, you could hear them coming as the excitement built, past Foster Hall, the student center building; past the men's dorms, making the right turn at the circle. The dorms would empty out, the three men's and three women's dorms, even the laundry mat. Students would leave their laundry and come out to the block.

Student's would stop eating or finish eating quickly to get out on the block because the band was coming, and we knew that the party was on. You know the block was where we hung out, everybody was there on the block.

Then President Carpenter asked Pam to tell her about Tidewater Slim… Again, a giddy elation of excitement swelled and filled her voice as she said that he had been in the band and had been in other area college marching bands.

He didn't live in the dorm. We didn't know if he lived or where he lived off campus. He was mysterious. Some say he was a warlock as he could disappear and show up unnoticed.

Tidewater Slim was unique in that if you were from Tidewater, that is Norfolk, Portsmouth, Suffolk, Hampton, Chesapeake, Virginia Beach, or Newport News, Tidewater Slim knew you and knew something about you, your family or high school, etc. He would walk right up to you with an easy greeting, calling you Home Girl or Home Boy. You won't find him in any of the year books, he won't be there.

I'm glad I was there at Virginia State when the Marching 110 would come through campus. After the football game they would put on another show across from the girl's dorm, and all the girls would come out. Each section in the band had their own groove and sectional show.

Yeah, the "Legendary-1970s Marching 110"…

THEY WERE THE THING!!!

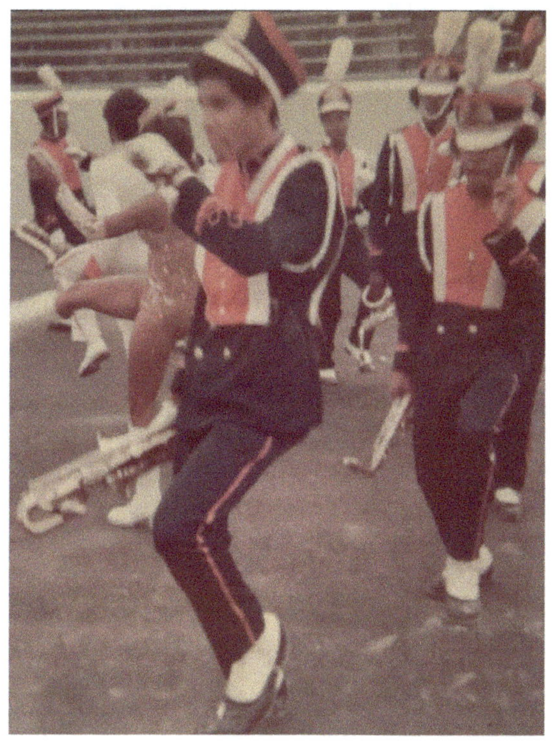

Wow!! It's great to see my Alma Mater continues to "high-step" and be recognized for it's musical & marching excellence!! I'll always carry with me (along with my Baritone Sax) the glory of having marched in the "VSU, Marching 110", "HAIL STATE!!!"

Marching behind me is our line brother, Bro. Wilson Everette!! Carrying his Alto Sax.

Couldn't keep that hat on!! Too Kool!!!

Circa 1974!!!!

William Taylor/Tate

We used to watch Cradock and Norcom perform in parades, when you were snare drumming. I remember Edward Williams (Bonehead) on the front row with his Trombone marching beside, Mr. Barkely, you alls director. Norcom was always the last band to complete the parade. Because they were the best or because they were all Black? I never knew why! From My Brother, Stephen J. Cox. March 2025

Milton Lawrence Cox II